Best Denver Trails

for HIKERS, FAMILIES, RUNNERS, & DOG LOVERS

Pamela Irwin

WESTCLIFFE PUBLISHERS
www.bigearthpublishing.com

Dedication

To our amazing children, for their love of the outdoors.

BRETT *backpacker, skier, & marathoner*

ANNE *serious bicyclist, teacher, & marathoner*

KELLY *artist, hiker, & gardener*

ISBN: 978-1-56579-633-1

EDITOR: Ali Geiser
DESIGNER: Rebecca Finkel

PUBLISHED BY:
Westcliffe Publishers,
a Big Earth Publishing company
1637 Pearl Street, Suite 201
Boulder, Colorado 80302

PRINTED IN China

9 8 7 6 5 4 3 2 1

Library of Congress Cataloging-in-Publication Data:
CIP DATA on file.

COVER PHOTO Runner image by akunamatata;
Dog image by Tudor

For more information about other fine books and calendars from Westcliffe Publishers, a Big Earth Publishing company, please contact your local bookstore, call us at 1-800-258-5830, or visit us on the Web at **bigearthpublishing.com**.

PLEASE NOTE: Risk is always a factor in mountain travel. The activities described in this book can be dangerous, especially when weather is adverse and when unforeseen events or conditions create a hazardous situation. The author has done her best to provide the reader with accurate information about mountain travel, as well as to point out some of its potential hazards. It is the responsibility of the users of this guide to learn the necessary skills for safe mountain travel, and to exercise caution in potentially hazardous areas. The author and publisher disclaim any liability for injury or other damage caused by any activity described in this book.

The author and publisher of this book have made every effort to ensure the accuracy of its information. Nevertheless, books can require revisions. Please feel free to let us know if you find information in this book that needs to be updated, and we will be glad to correct it for the next printing. Your comments and suggestions are always welcome.

Contents

Introduction

There are 10,000 miles of trail in Colorado. Those convenient to the Denver metro area offer a diverse array of scenery, terrain, flora, and fauna. It is with you in mind that the best of these trails have been gathered into this carry-along guide.

The trails chosen for this handy little volume represent everything from level walks perfect for families, to foothills jaunts, to montane adventures. It's up to you to choose hikes that appeal to your time constraints, desire, and capability. To help you get the most out of this guide, we've included

symbols that will let you know at a glance if the trail is kid-friendly, dog-friendly, or good for running.

Though Denver is sometimes called "Queen City of the Plains," it is more mountain-oriented as far as outdoor recreation goes. Visitors and residents alike lift their eyes to the Front Range of the Rockies that backdrop the city. With this handy guide, you are set to discover, explore, and enjoy the region's plains and mountains alike.

Satisfaction comes with the territory as you exercise your body as well as your mind. So pick a trail, dress appropriately, and don't forget that Denver is the Mile-High City, making water supply, sun protection, and weather-wise gear imperative. Note that fees are levied at some venues, mainly state parks.

Welcome to a great opportunity to enjoy the power of being out there, while finding out what makes Denver's Front Range region so alluring.

—PAM IRWIN

Wheat Ridge Greenbelt

Distance 3.0 miles

Difficulty Easy

Elevation Gain Negligible

Dogs On leash

Directions From Denver, take 1-25 north to 1-70 W towards Grand Junction. Continue 7.5 miles on 1-70, then exit at CO 391 S/Kipling St. Turn left onto Kipling St., then right (east) onto W. 41st St. Trailhead is 0.3 mile ahead where road ends.

Highlights Ponds; picnic tables; wildlife; butterflies; fishing opportunities; habitat garden

WHY NOT...

Pack a delicious picnic backpack full of goodies! Try a nice loaf of crusty bread, an assortment of tasty cheeses, fruit, and, for a special treat, chocolate. For refreshments, try sparkling cider or your favorite juice.

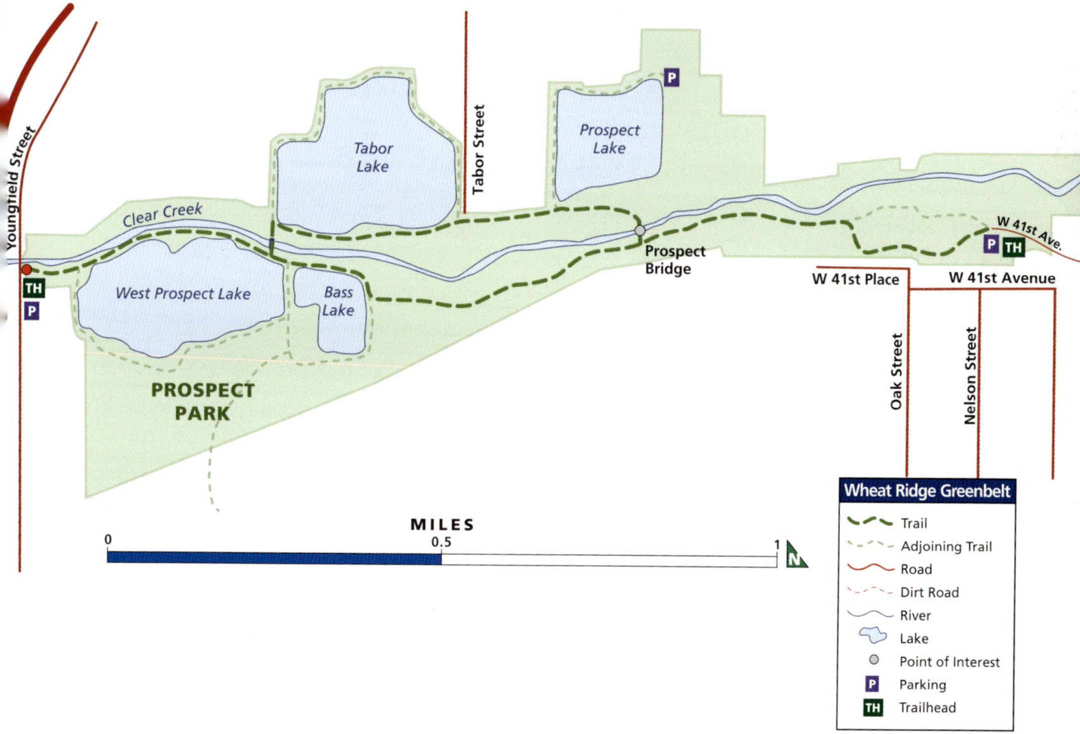
Youngfield Street
Clear Creek
Tabor Lake
Tabor Street
Prospect Lake
West Prospect Lake
Bass Lake
Prospect Bridge
W 41st Ave.
W 41st Place
W 41st Avenue
Oak Street
Nelson Street
PROSPECT PARK
TH
P
MILES
0
0.5
1
N
Wheat Ridge Greenbelt
Trail
Adjoining Trail
Road
Dirt Road
River
Lake
Point of Interest
Parking
Trailhead

Metro-close Wheat Ridge Greenbelt invites you to delve into a bit of suburban wilderness. This is a place of birdsong and creek sounds. Several small lakes may deliver lucky anglers with largemouth and smallmouth bass. Covered picnic tables are placed here and there along the way. The greenbelt is suitable for hikers or bikers.

The **Miller Trailhead** of Wheat Ridge Greenbelt serves both the crusher-fines hiking trail and the concrete bike path. Take the left fork to begin on the wide, natural-surfaced trail. You'll soon rejoin the bike path. Summer visitors will find this trail flanked by lots of milkweed, the primary food source for monarch butterfly larvae; look for the orange and black-winged adults. Travel under mature cottonwoods, willows, and box elders. Birds and foxes frequent this wild-in-the-city place. Occasional patches of poison ivy appear off the trail.

To your right, a pre-rusted arc (Prospect Bridge—the bridge upon which this balloon loop returns) spans Clear Creek to access Prospect Park. For now, continue straight ahead on the south side of the stream. Shortly, you'll reach Bass Lake, edged by an extensive cattail zone. As you approach the water, look for a bench hiding behind a tall patch of feather reed grass—this is a good place to watch for fish jumping and waterfowl flying.

Continue west along the north shore of Bass Lake, then along West Prospect Lake. Pass another attractive bridge where the bike path merges with our trail. The path changes to hard surface and cruises west to reach Youngfield Street trailhead parking, where restrooms are available.

After checking the map sign, retrace your steps eastward along West Prospect Lake, watching for big blue herons, cormorants, and other waterbirds. When you arrive at the first bridge over Clear Creek, cross the span to access Tabor Lake. Sharing the bike path now, turn right, along this lake's open south shore.

Shaded once again, the path reaches the west side of Prospect Park. If you still have energy, take a left to enjoy a small habitat garden, entered by an arbor. Return on a path bisecting the park and head east toward Prospect Lake. A fishing float offers a nice view of the water. In front of the picnic pavilion, Prospect Bridge takes you back across the creek. Turn to the left and retrace your steps back to the parking area.

Van Bibber Park

Van Bibber Creek/Jimmy Go

Distance	2.0-mile loop
Difficulty	Easy
Elevation Gain	Negligible
Dogs	On leash
Directions	From Denver, take I-70 west to exit 266/Ward Road. Turn right onto Ward Rd. and continue about 1.3 miles to reach Van Bibber Park on your left (west).
Highlights	Wetlands; creek; picnic area

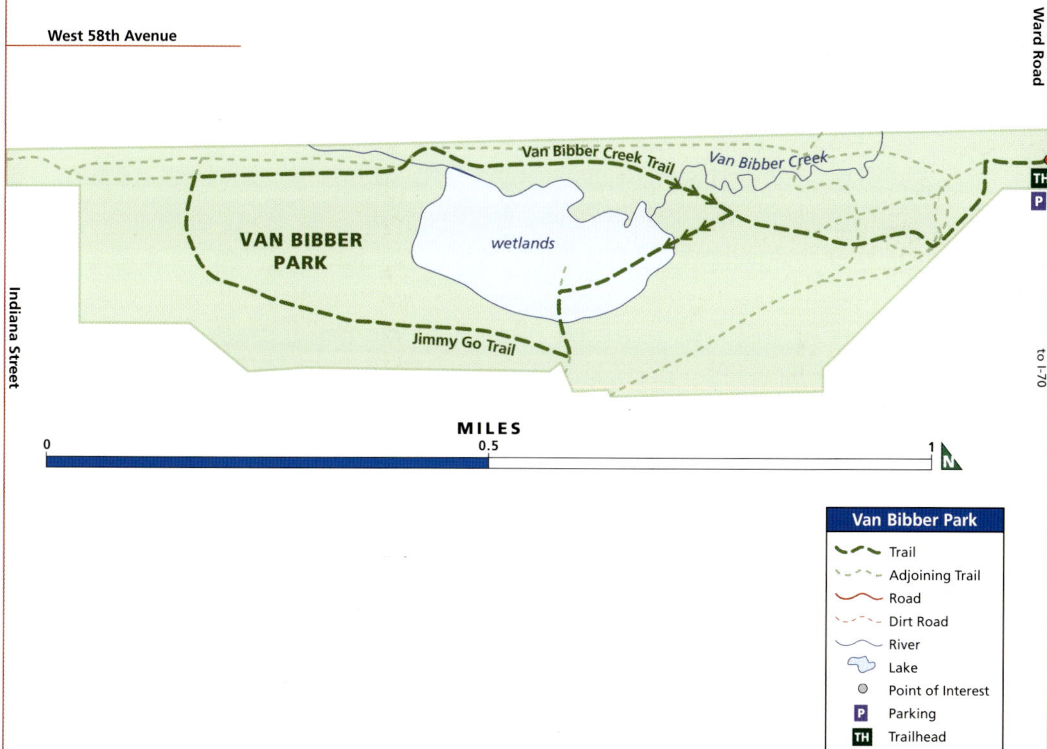

West 58th Avenue
Ward Road
Indiana Street
Van Bibber Creek Trail
Van Bibber Creek
VAN BIBBER PARK
wetlands
Jimmy Go Trail
TH
P
to I-70
MILES
0
0.5
1
N
Van Bibber Park
Trail
Adjoining Trail
Road
Dirt Road
River
Lake
Point of Interest
Parking
Trailhead

Van Bibber Park, described as "A green home right in the city," is a peaceful pocket of grasslands and wetlands. This Jefferson County Open Space Park is secreted down in a vale worn by little Van Bibber Creek.

Walkers, rollerbladers, and bicyclists enjoy the gentle, winding concrete pathways. Additionally, a 2-mile, natural-surfaced trail loops through the central wetlands area. Benches and picnic tables offer rest. Maps are available near the trailhead information sign.

From the parking area, head west towards the restrooms. Walk through a variety of grasses to go left on hikers-only **Van Bibber Creek Trail.** A horse trail takes off to the right.

Head briefly uphill and south before turning west again. Keep straight at the next intersection. Shortly after, you'll reach another—go left on **Jimmy Go Trail.** Van Bibber Creek Trail, on which you will return, goes right. The nearby wetland's observation deck is a handy platform to observe a tiny jigsaw-puzzle-piece pond and listen for the gargling warble of red-winged blackbirds.

Sedges and cattails on the uphill side indicate moist pockets, and fine foothill views lead you west. The path heads south briefly, reaching an intersection. Take a hard right to continue west. The path then turns north towards a squiggly line of cottonwoods; follow the trail as it bends to the right. Shaded by cottonwoods where squirrels play, a picnic table appears for a snack attack.

Take a right to rejoin Van Bibber Creek Trail, heading east. You'll cross little Van Bibber Creek. About half way back to the parking area along a yucca studded hillock, a slight rise features a bench overlooking a riparian zone of willow and cattails, just the place to rest and identify the throaty warble of red-winged blackbirds. Crossing the creek again ushers in a pair of picnic shelters. You'll soon retrace the string of the balloon loop to return to the parking area.

Fun 4 Kids!

Male red-winged blackbird's shoulder patches appear all bright red, but keen-eyed kids may discover the yellow band as well. What does the song sound like in words? Can you discern more than one call?

Cherry Creek State Park

East Wetlands Preserve Loop

Distance 1.2-mile balloon loop

Difficulty Easy

Elevation Gain Negligible

Dogs Not permitted

Directions From Denver, take 1-25 south towards Colorado Springs. Take exit 200 to merge onto 1-225 N and go 4 miles. Take exit 4 to merge onto CO 83 S/S Parker Rd. and go 1.4 miles. Turn right (west) to enter the Cherry Creek State Park east entrance. Go 0.8 mile, and then turn left. Go 0.2 mile, then take another left and go 0.5 mile to reach Shop Creek Trailhead on your right.

Fees & Info Yearly Colorado State Parks Pass $60. Day pass $8 May 1st–September 30th; $7 October 1st–April 30th. For more information, call (303) 690-1166.

Highlights Abundant wildlife; swimming and boating opportunities nearby; wetland habitat

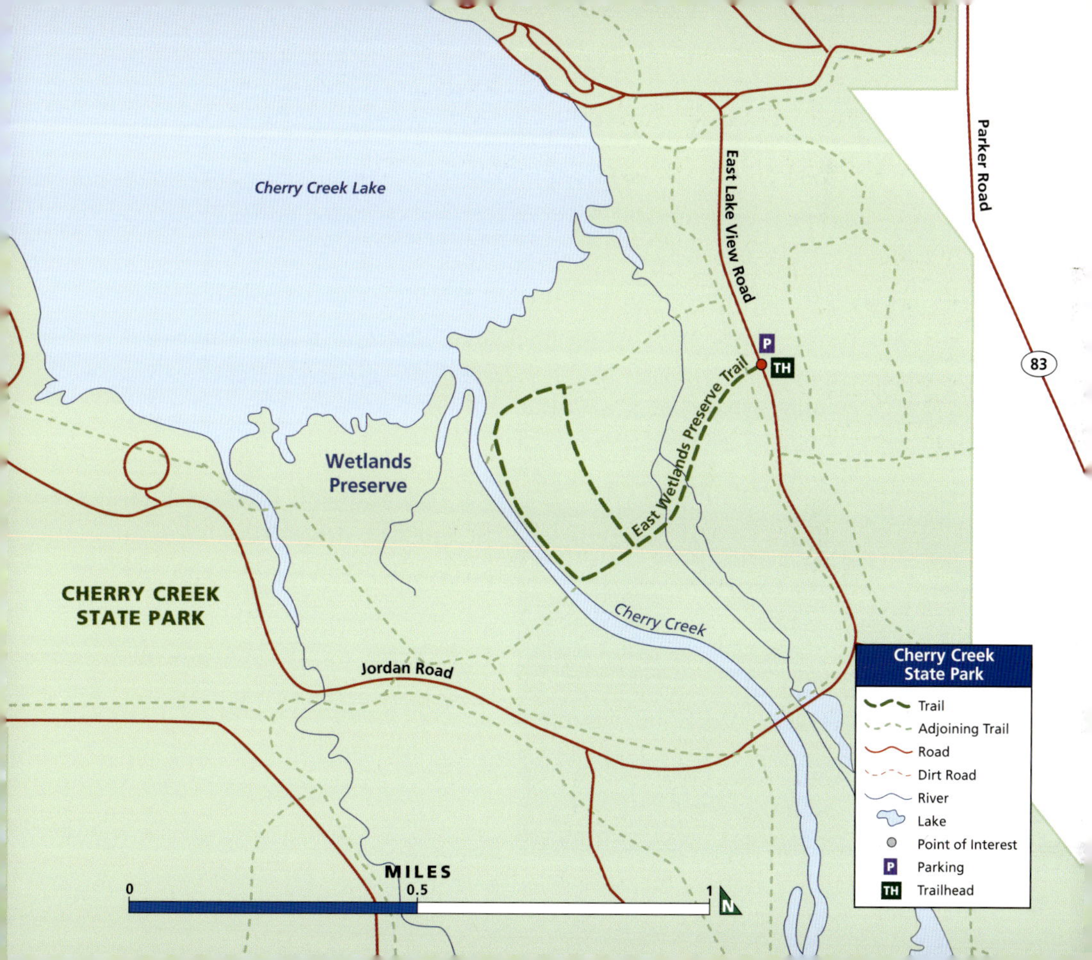

Cherry Creek Lake
Wetlands Preserve
CHERRY CREEK STATE PARK
East Lake View Road
Parker Road
83
P
TH
East Wetlands Preserve Trail
Cherry Creek
Jordan Road
MILES
0
0.5
1
N
Cherry Creek State Park
Trail
Adjoining Trail
Road
Dirt Road
River
Lake
Point of Interest
Parking
Trailhead

With over 3,900 acres, including an 880-acre reservoir, Cherry Creek State Park deserves its popularity. The East Wetlands Preserve loop, enhanced by a veritable forest of cottonwood trees, provides a place to study nature and make discoveries.

This easy 1.2-mile trail offers bird and wildlife watching opportunities. Come early while fauna is active. It's a good idea to pick up a map at the entry station or park offices. No bikes or dogs are allowed in this preserve.

From the peeled log rail fence at the parking lot, turn left onto the **East Wetlands Preserve Trail.** It quickly drops you onto a boardwalk. Kids might be excited by the minuscule pond patched with diminutive duckweed. Continue past a colorful interpretive sign.

A gate welcomes you into a wildlife discovery zone. Keep your eyes open for whitetail deer and cottontail rabbits. The canopy is alive with birds such as Bullocks orioles, western wood peewees, and goldfinches, each singing a unique song. This willow-walled trail, labeled **S-1,** constitutes the string of the balloon loop.

Cross a footbridge, after which the understory thickens. At a junction, take a sharp turn to the right (north). The wide path may introduce birds denizens such as yellow warblers, evening grosbeaks, and the familiar American robin. An open meadow beckons, and the trail winds around to bring you a view of Cherry Creek Dam. The path then turns south, narrowing as it reenters woods. The cattail marsh on the right is a good place to watch for butterflies and dragonflies. Pass through a grassy meadow. High willows once again flank the path. Turn right (east) to rejoin the string of the balloon loop and head back to the parking area.

Did You Know...

The Cherry Creek Dam was the first of three dams built to protect Denver from the devastating floodwaters of the South Platte River. The floods were a problem in Denver for over 100 years before the dam was finished. Construction was completed in 1950. The dam also provides irrigation to the surrounding areas.

Barr Lake

Boardwalk Gazebo and Niedrach Nature Trail

Distance 2.6 miles out and back, plus boardwalk

Difficulty Easy

Elevation Gain Negligible

Dogs Not permitted

Directions From Denver, take I-25 north to I-76. Head east on I-76, continuing for about 16 miles. Exit towards Bromley Ln., heading right on E 152nd Ave. Continue about a mile, then go right on Picadilly Rd; the Barr Lake State Park entrance is on right. Park in the south lot, near the nature center.

Fees & Info Yearly Colorado State Parks Pass $60; day pass $6. Niedrach Nature Trail is closed Monday and Thursday. For more information, call (303) 659-6005.

Highlights Abundant wildlife; large reservoir; great birding venue; mountain views; wildlife observation blinds

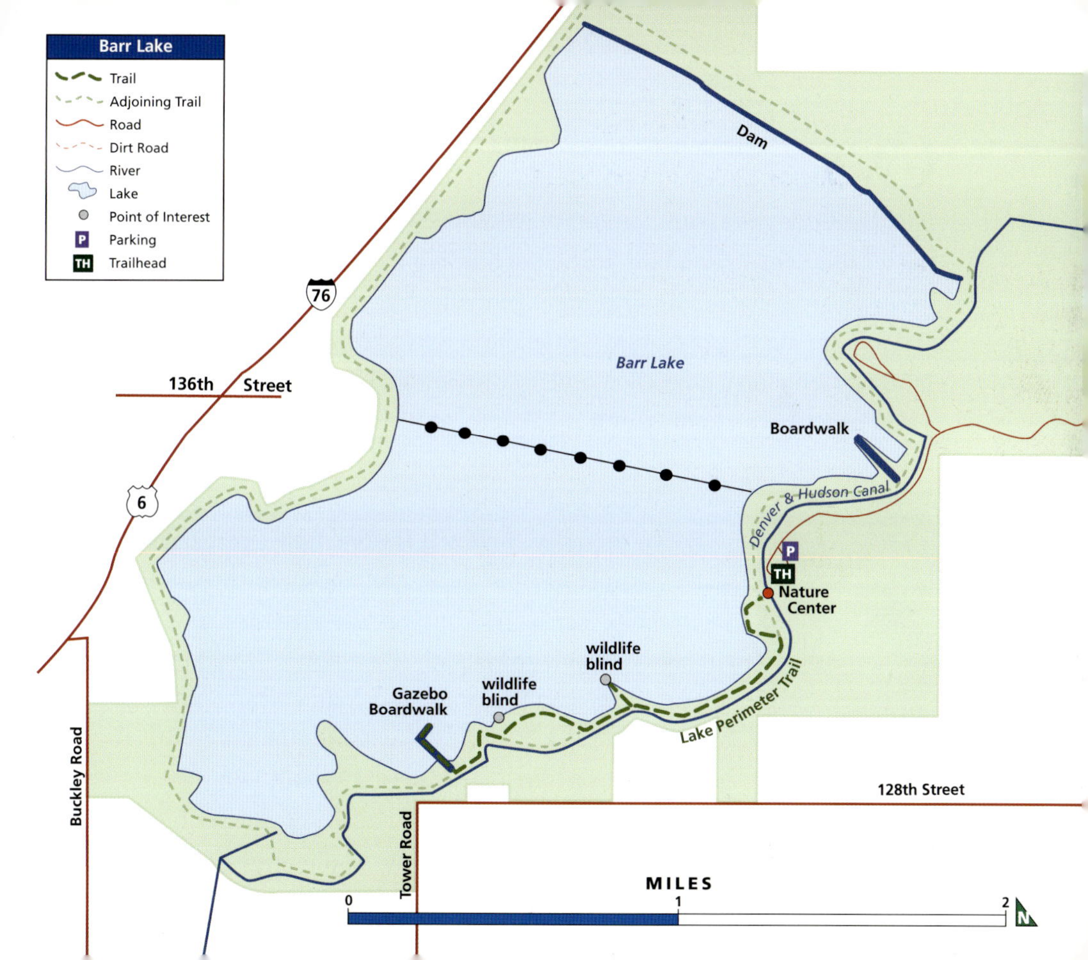

Barr Lake
Trail
Adjoining Trail
Road
Dirt Road
River
Lake
Point of Interest
Parking
Trailhead
76
136th Street
6
Buckley Road
Dam
Barr Lake
Boardwalk
Denver & Hudson Canal
P
TH
Nature Center
wildlife blind
wildlife blind
Gazebo Boardwalk
Lake Perimeter Trail
128th Street
Tower Road
MILES
0
1
2
N

Of the 2,700-plus acres that comprise Barr Lake State Park, the reservoir takes up over 1,900. Sitting on the prairie northeast of Denver, Barr Lake is a great place to observe wildlife, especially birds. Check with the visitors center for a bird list before heading for the flat, 1.3-mile trail to the Boardwalk Gazebo. Parking is generous.

From the Barr Lake Nature Center, head west, crossing the Denver and Hudson Canal on a pre-rusted bridge. Turn left on **Lake Perimeter Trail**—a sign here lets you know that it is 1.3 miles to the Boardwalk Gazebo. Big cottonwoods rise on the right—there may be a bird or two in them that you can check off the list.

Soon, the nifty **Niedrach Nature Trail**—part boardwalk, part observation deck, and anchored by colorful interpretive signs—beckons on the right. Follow the timber-confined, gravel path. Remount the boardwalk, now elevated over wetlands, and follow it to a covered observation deck. Check for wildlife, then shift your gaze to the west for a view of 14,259-foot Longs Peak.

The boardwalk returns you to the Lake Perimeter Trail. Head right, following the roadway past a bench or two. A short spur at the 1-mile mark accesses a wildlife observation station. This wooden blind stands in the shadow of giant cottonwoods. Another little detour takes you through Fox Meadow to reach another blind.

Winding levelly and passing open shoreline wetlands, the trail comes to a rail fence at the 1.3-mile point. Turn right and walk out on the boardwalk—it carries you above the lake's surfaces and stretches for 250 yards, doglegging among islands of willow on its way to the roomy observation gazebo.

The sturdy, eight-sided gazebo sports benches around half its perimeter. Skim the lake's surface and perimeter for waterfowl and shorebirds. Though the bald eagles' nest for which Barr Lake became famous blew down in a storm, the same pair built a new nest. If you should spot a big bird with flat outstretched wings and a white head, you may be observing a mature bald eagle.

Fun 4 Kids!

Your children are the next generation of wildlife enthusiasts and protectors. Be sure to teach them good exploring techniques that can help preserve the environment. Barr Lake is a great example of an environment that has been maintained and cared for. With bald eagles nesting there and over 350 bird species having been sighted, it is a wonderful place to encourage an appreciative love for nature.

Carson Nature Center

Northern Wildlife Loop

Distance	1.4-mile balloon loop
Difficulty	Easy
Elevation Gain	Negligible
Dogs	On 6-foot leash
Directions	From Denver, head south on 1-25. Go south on US 85. Head right on Mineral Ave., then take your next right onto South Platte River Parkway. Take the first left and continue to the visitors center parking lot.
Highlights	Nature programs; Carson Nature Center; waterfowl viewing

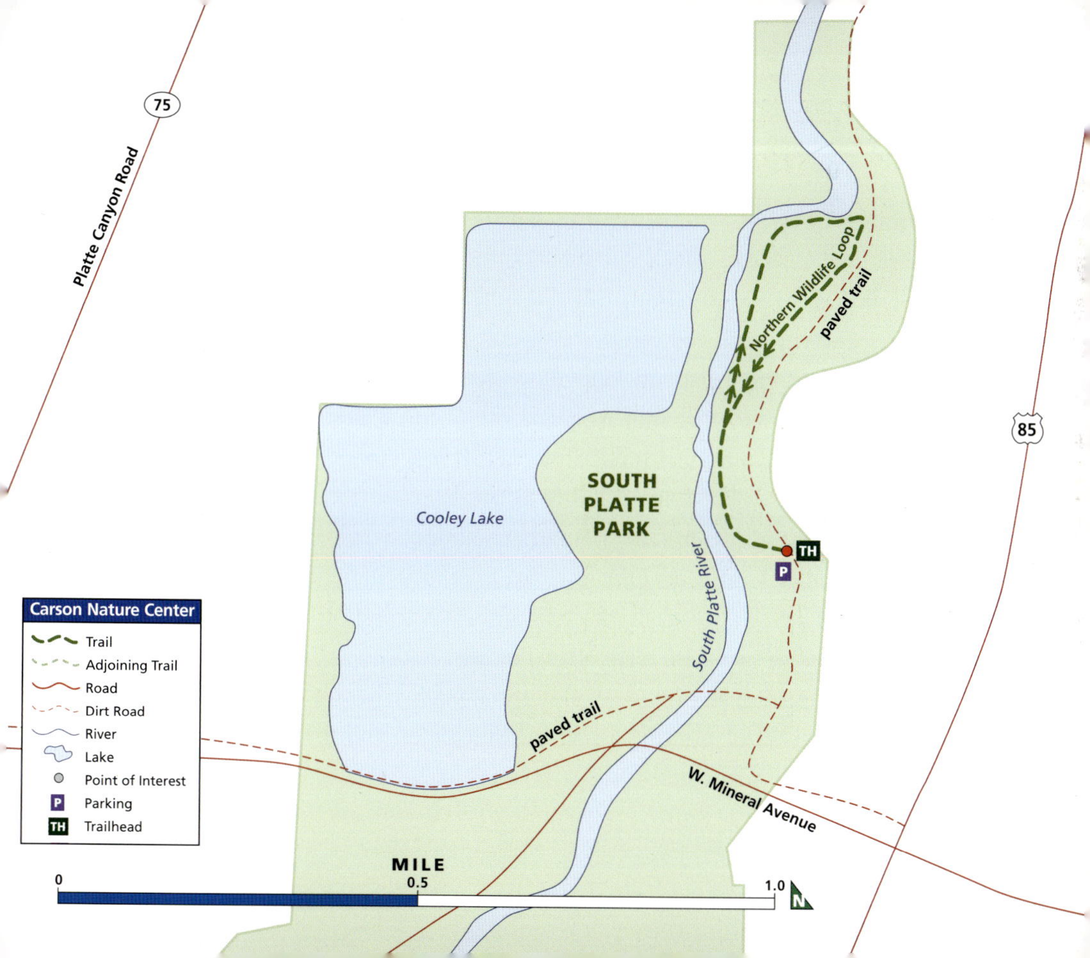

75
Platte Canyon Road
85
Cooley Lake
SOUTH PLATTE PARK
South Platte River
Northern Wildlife Loop
paved trail
paved trail
TH
P
W. Mineral Avenue
Carson Nature Center
Trail
Adjoining Trail
Road
Dirt Road
River
Lake
Point of Interest
Parking
Trailhead
MILE
0
0.5
1.0
N

The Carson Nature Center, located near the trailhead, is a great place for kids to check out before setting off to explore the Northern Wildlife Loop. A wide variety of nature-oriented programs are offered there, and kids can check out their tanks of native fish, snakes, and turtles. For more information, call (303)730-1022. Parking for the nature center and the trailhead can be competitive on weekends.

This convenient balloon loop allows for close-up viewing of the waterfowl and wading birds that frequent the South Platte River. With little elevation change, the natural surface trail is easygoing for little legs.

To access the **Northern Wildlife Loop,** head north from the trailhead information sign on a concrete pathway. Soon, you'll turn right, onto a narrow, natural-surfaced path that veers off the main Platte Greenway's concrete sidewalk to reach the embankment standing above the South Platte River. A sign here reads: "river access."

Willow bushes lead the way along the water where mallards and other ducks dabble. Look out for cousins big blue heron and the smaller, less-seen black-crowned night heron.

Drift down to reach a fork that begins the balloon portion of the nature loop. Head left towards the river, your route confirmed by an arrow on a post.

Where you pass above the river on an abrupt embankment, look below for Canada geese and ducks that like to congregate on sand spits. Ahead, exposed snags rise above a big tree on the far bank, a favorite spot of cormorants. Nearby, dragonflies hover only to dart away.

Wend your way through jungle-like vegetation, such as wild hop vine, to continue to where the river bends and the path crosses a sturdy timber spanning a bit of clear water. Big patriarch cottonwoods mark the place where the loop takes a strong right and heads for a little footbridge. Another turn to the right keeps you on the loop as you head south under trees.

Fun 4 Kids!

Bring along a pair of binoculars so that kids can view the Front Range and spot wildlife along the trail. See how many different types of animals you can observe along the hike. Be sure to use caution when near wild animals, and do not feed or approach the wildlife.

Watch for a nice view of the Front Range in the distant west as you aim back to rejoin the string of the balloon loop you have now completed, ready to retrace your steps back to the parking lot.

Roxborough State Park

Willow Creek Loop

Distance	1.4-mile loop
Difficulty	Easy
Elevation Gain	100 feet
Dogs	Not permitted
Directions	From Denver, take I-25 west to CO 470 east. Exit onto CO 121/South Wadsworth Blvd. Turn left onto Waterton Rd., then right onto North Rampart Range Rd. Turn left at North Roxborough Park Rd., then right onto Roxborough Dr.
Fees & Info	Yearly Colorado State Parks Pass $60; day pass $6. For more information, call (303) 973-3959.
Highlights	Dramatic rock formations; creek

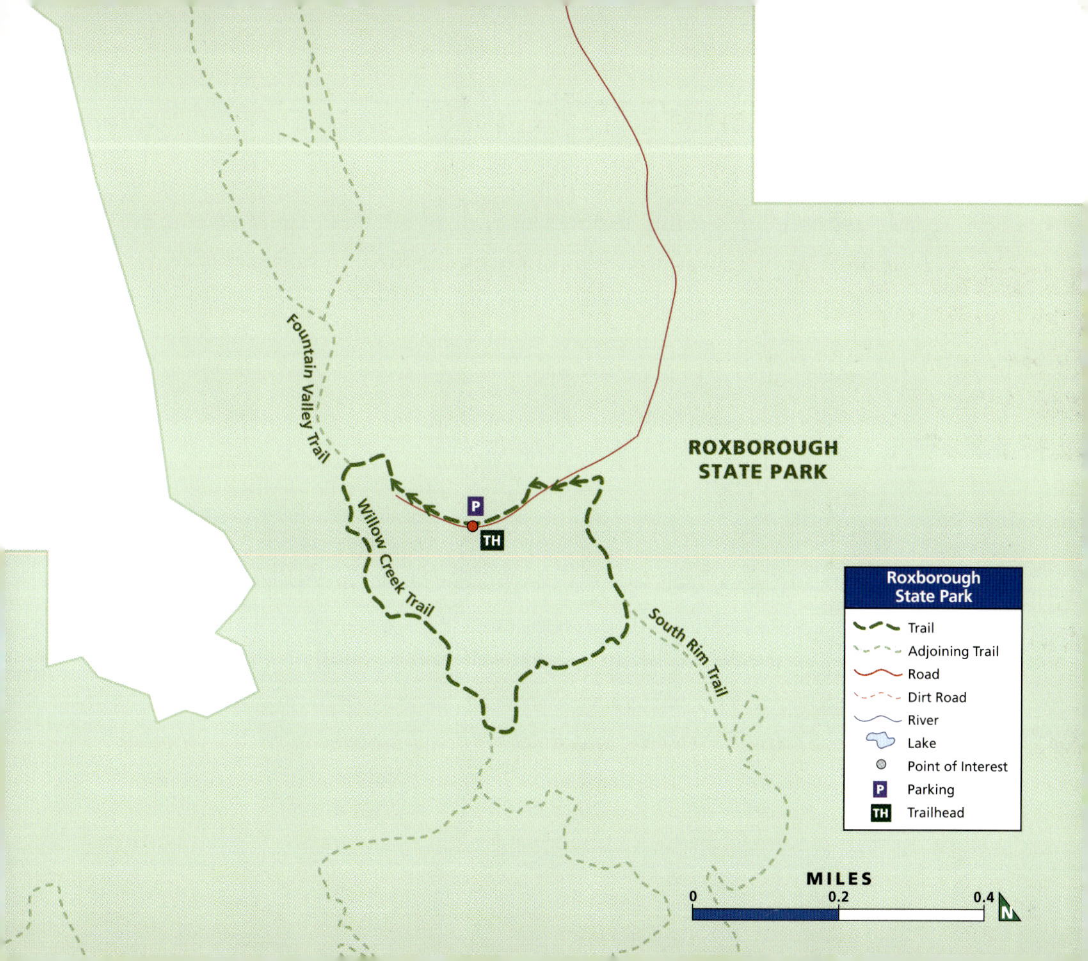
Fountain Valley Trail
Willow Creek Trail
South Rim Trail
P
TH
ROXBOROUGH STATE PARK
Roxborough State Park
Trail
Adjoining Trail
Road
Dirt Road
River
Lake
Point of Interest
Parking
Trailhead
MILES
0
0.2
0.4
N

An excellent time to explore the trails of Roxborough State Park is early morning, when low-angled light on the rock formations is memorable and wildlife viewing is optimal. Kids of all ages gaze in awe at the towering fins of 300-million-year-old red sandstone. In the visitors center, you'll find interactive exhibits and a bookstore. Roxborough offers a full slate of scheduled visitor activities, many created with the younger generations in mind.

Parking is in paved lots, which may fill on fine-weather weekends. Try an early weekday morning instead. Early birds may avoid summer afternoon thunderstorms.

West of the visitors center's flagstone patio, a sign directs you to 1.4-mile **Willow Creek Trail,** the shortest in the park. Immediately entering scrub oak, the shaded path soon encounters a sign: "leaves of three, leave them be," which warns of the presence of poison ivy trailside in the first 0.25 mile.

The trail heads for views and wildflowers. An opening with a wooden bench faces east, toward the Lyons Formation's ancient petrified sand dunes. Direct your view further east, to the Dakota Hogback's solidified lagoonal mud layers, which were laid down in the age of dinosaurs.

Continue along the level trail. A small footbridge aims the route slightly up, exposing rock formation views. The trail crunches underfoot as you approach a junction where our Willow Creek loop follows the left fork. Drop gently through scrub oak to cross an open meadow. Drift down to a child-sized footbridge spanning a tiny stream. Linger near the bridge to check out the prehistoric horsetails growing by the waterway. Directly ahead is a bench by a stand of willows flanking trickling Willow Creek.

After meandering through scrub oak, the trail emerges into the open. Soon a bench-anchored junction arrives, and our loop goes left again, descending through bushes and more scrub oak. Cross a railed bridge and continue straight ahead. The path parallels the entrance road and crosses it before reaching the parking lot.

Fun 4 Kids!

Take advantage of ample opportunities to learn from the Roxborough Park naturalists who love answering your children's questions. Also be sure to check out the programs available for your kids in this area, including those on the patio featuring skulls, skins, and mega-fauna headgear. Puppets and story time dates are offered as well.

Lookout Mountain

Forest Loop

Distance	0.6-mile loop
Difficulty	Easy
Elevation Gain	80 feet
Dogs	Not permitted
Directions	From Denver, take I-70 west to exit 256. Follow the brown highway signs to Lookout Mountain.
Highlights	Green-built nature center; ponderosa pine forest

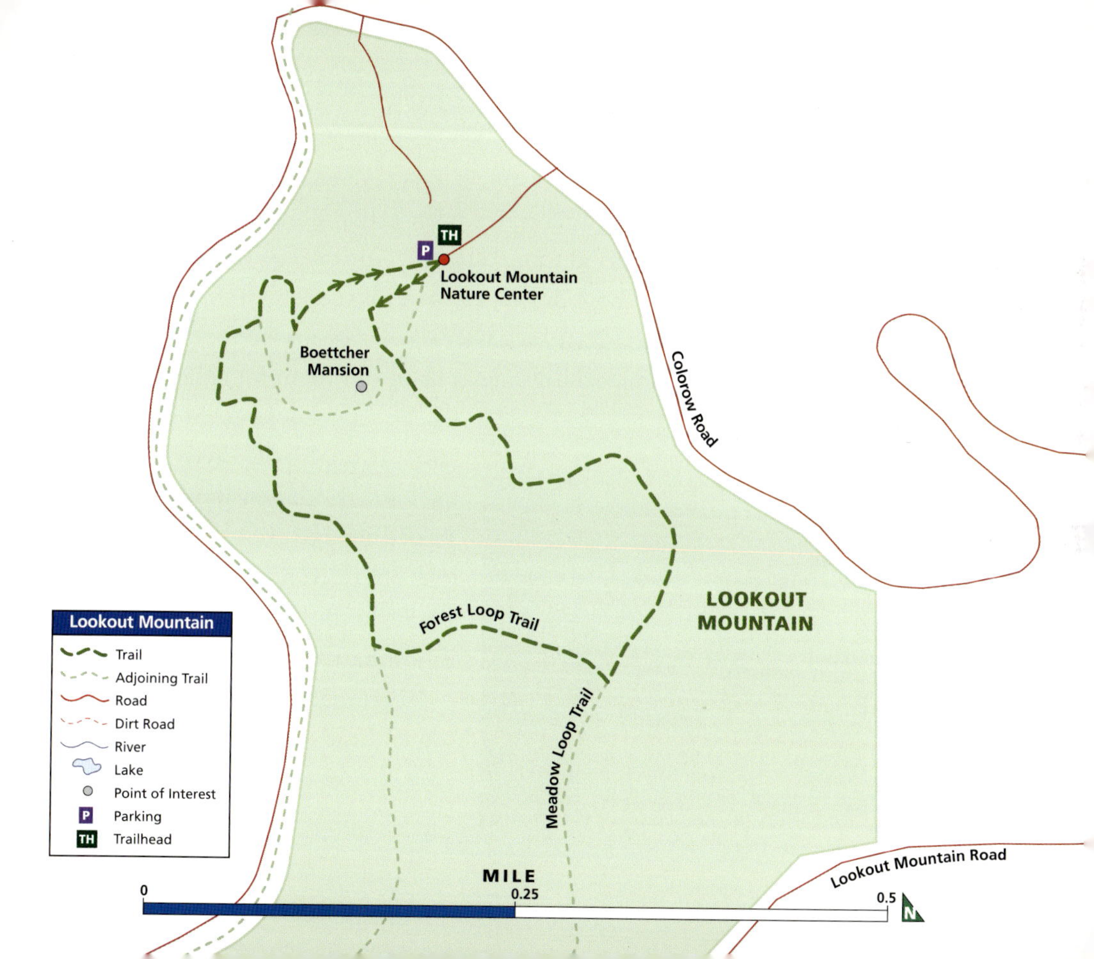

Lookout Mountain
Trail
Adjoining Trail
Road
Dirt Road
River
Lake
Point of Interest
Parking
Trailhead
TH
P
Lookout Mountain Nature Center
Boettcher Mansion
Colorow Road
LOOKOUT MOUNTAIN
Forest Loop Trail
Meadow Loop Trail
Lookout Mountain Road
MILE
0
0.25
0.5
N

Perched on top of Lookout Mountain west of Golden, Lookout Mountain Nature Center and Preserve is a great venue for families and nature lovers. The first-rate nature center is an extraordinarily beautiful example of a building constructed using earth-friendly materials. Recycled train boxcars, soda bottles, and windshields were all used in creating this building that has been aptly described as "Elegance of nature recycled." The center houses interesting exhibits and a hands-on room for children.

Check out Lookout Mountain's naturalist-led activities for kids. Parking in the pine-shaded lot becomes competitive on weekends as well as when the Boettcher Mansion is hosting an event.

Beginning from the nature center, head south on a shaded path toward the imposing

Boettcher Mansion. Bear left of some picnic tables to find a map board featuring 0.6-mile **Forest Loop Trail.** Note that you can link onto the **Meadow Loop Trail** for a longer hike.

Dominated by ponderosa pines, Forest Loop curves south of the Tudor-style Boettcher mansion, until a junction turns the route left. As you wander along the pine-flanked path you might be fortunate enough to spot the elusive Abert's squirrel. This dark, often black, tuft-eared squirrel is most likely to be seen under or in his room-and-board tree, the long-needled ponderosa pine.

The smooth path now comes to a footbridge where a sign says "Meadow Loop." Keep right unless you plan on Meadow Loop's extra 0.8 mile. You'll pass another junction where Meadow Loop rejoins Forest Loop. Again, keep right. The loop leads back toward the nature center.

Trail Runner's Checklist

- Trail-specific shoes with good tread
- Lightweight, breathable jacket
- Lightweight gloves
- Sunglasses
- Hydration pack or belt and energy gels or bars

Evergreen Lake Loop

Distance 1.0-mile loop

Difficulty Easy

Elevation Gain 40 feet

Dogs On leash

Directions From Denver, take I-70 west to Evergreen Parkway/CO 74 E. Exit south to Upper Bear Creek Rd. Go about 0.3 mile, then take a left to reach the parking area for Evergreen Lake.

Highlights Nearby boat rentals and golf course; wetlands; diverse and exciting trail; waterfowl sighting opportunities; fishing opportunities; xeric garden

74
74
Upper Bear Creek Road
Upper Bear Creek
marshy area
Evergreen Lake
Bear Creek
Lake House
boathouse
73
Wilmot Creek
Cub Creek
Evergreen Lake Loop
Trail
Adjoining Trail
Road
Dirt Road
River
Lake
Point of Interest
Parking
Trailhead
P
TH
MILES
0
0.1
0.2
N

In summer, a leisurely rental boat paddle on Evergreen Lake's dancing waters is a perfect outing. Since the lake is surrounded by trees, a slice of golf course, wetlands, and a few picturesque structures, encircling the lake by foot via boardwalk, footbridge, natural surface pathways, and steel steps offers quite a diverse 1-mile excursion. And all this is central to old downtown Evergreen. Weekend parking in the paved lot is competitive.

Begin hiking from the imposing log lake house. Starting from the south side of the structure, head lakeside on crusher-fines toward a vintage boardwalk, passing the old boathouse.

As you continue eastward next to the water, watch for waterfowl paddling or sunning. The adjacent riparian-influenced bank, accessed by a wide boardwalk, is ideal for fishermen or families.

Arcing gracefully, a metal bridge lifts you to continue your walk around the south shore. An angled boardwalk cum fishing deck, replete with inviting built-in benches, suggests a fine rest stop.

Curve northerly along an outcrop wall where the path skips through ponderosa pine shade. Prepare to mount a set of steel stairs; descend on the far side to a footbridge spanning spillway waters. Pause at a replica of a Frederic Remington mountain man on horseback statue before crossing a short bridge to reach a circular demonstration garden of xeric plants.

The garden path rejoins the main route to cross over Bear Creek. Ascend some more stairs, then cruise west and drop to lake level. Alder-studded wetlands may harbor mallard ducks, big blue herons, and black cormorants. Pleasantly level, the trail bends left to another arced bridge, followed by a boardwalk. Bisecting cattail wetlands beloved of gargling, red-winged blackbirds, the loop now heads back to the parking lots.

Local Scene

After exploring Evergreen Lake, reward yourself with an ice cream cone. Relax streamside with your treat and then explore more of the historic town of Evergreen.

Pine Valley Ranch

Pine Lake/North Fork View/Narrow Gauge

Distance 1.5-mile loop

Difficulty Easy

Elevation Gain Negligible

Dogs On leash

Directions From Denver, take I-70 west. Take exit 260 to go east on CO 470. Exit onto US 285 S. Turn left at Pine Valley Rd./CO 126 and continue approximately 6 miles. Head right on Crystal Lake Rd. to reach entry gate for Pine Valley Ranch Open Space.

Highlights South Platte River; star-watching at nearby observatory; plentiful picnic sites; fishing opportunities at lake and along river; trail follows an old railroad track

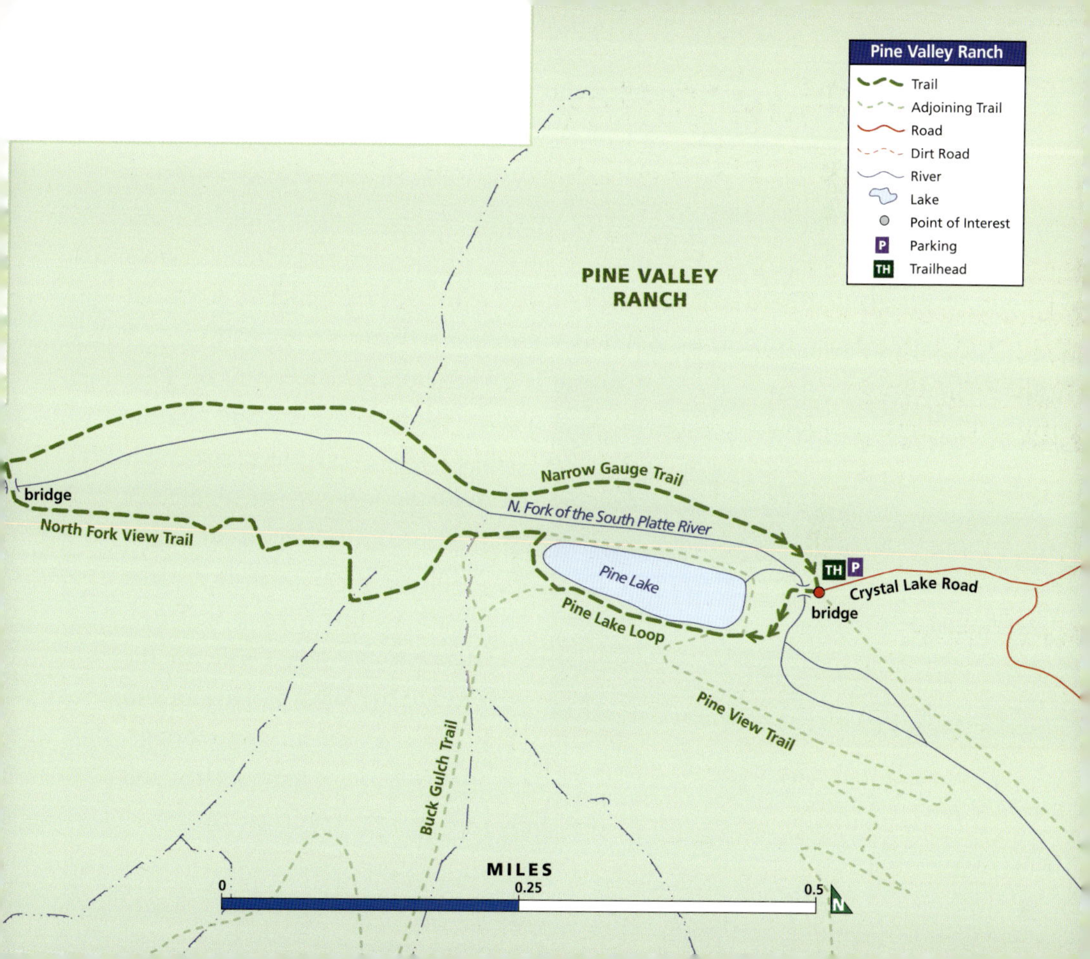

Pine Valley Ranch
Trail
Adjoining Trail
Road
Dirt Road
River
Lake
Point of Interest
P Parking
TH Trailhead
PINE VALLEY RANCH
Narrow Gauge Trail
N. Fork of the South Platte River
bridge
North Fork View Trail
TH
P
Crystal Lake Road
bridge
Pine Lake
Pine Lake Loop
Pine View Trail
Buck Gulch Trail
MILES
0
0.25
0.5
N

From towering spires of Colorado blue spruce to the clear North Fork of the South Platte River, Pine Valley Ranch Open Space Park has much to entice visitors. Cupped in a river-carved canyon, this Jefferson County Open Space Park offers pavilions, picnic sites, and a small fishable lake. Kids 10 and older can experience a scheduled star program at the old observatory, reached by climbing 0.4-mile Star View service road.

This loop, which travels on Pine Lake, North Fork View, and Narrow Gauge Trails is nearly level, making it great for young children and folks who like to saunter. Paved parking at the trailhead is on three levels; the topmost is set up for horse trailers.

To begin the loop, walk to the west end of the lower parking lot and cross the river on an arced bridge. Turn left onto a wide concrete pathway that will pass a stone shelter, and continue along the south shore of Pine Lake.

Regularly stocked with fish, this little lake offers grassy verges for anglers and loungers alike. A trio of fishing decks provide places to pause as does a bench fronting a slope ravaged by wildfire. **Park View Trail** heads off to the left; stay right on **Pine Lake Loop.**

Coming around the west end of the lake, note a verdant wetland. Stay right at the next intersection. Soon after, you'll take a left onto hikers-only **North Fork View Trail.** The trail curves around westward into a scenic meadow, wending between hillside and riverside.

Cross a bridge spanning the peridot-green South Platte River to meet **Narrow Gauge Trail.** The route takes us right (east) and follows the 1878 railroad grade of the Denver, Leadville and Gunnison Railroad, installed to haul ice in the first decade of the 1900s. Pass by wildflowers, wild hops, and willows. As you return past Pine Lake, look between its north shore and the river to spot an old beaver lodge. Follow the trail back to the parking lot.

Why Not...

Pack a deli meal to eat in the gazebo while the South Platte River provides music. On certain nights, arrive for a star-filled sky-watch before attending the observatory evening program. For reservations, call Jeffco Open Space: 303-271-5925. For a great daytime activity, bring along a fishing rod. Pine Lake is regularly stocked with fish.

Red Rocks Park and Amphitheater Trading Post Loop

Distance	1.4-mile loop
Difficulty	Easy
Elevation Gain	200 feet
Dogs	On leash
Directions	From Denver, take 1-70 west to CO 470 south. Continue to exit 259/Morrison. Turn left and go 1.5 miles to the Red Rocks Park entrance. Go right for 1.1 miles on Red Rocks Dr., then take a left to reach the trading post.
Highlights	Dramatic red-rock outcrops; world-renowned Red Rocks Amphitheater

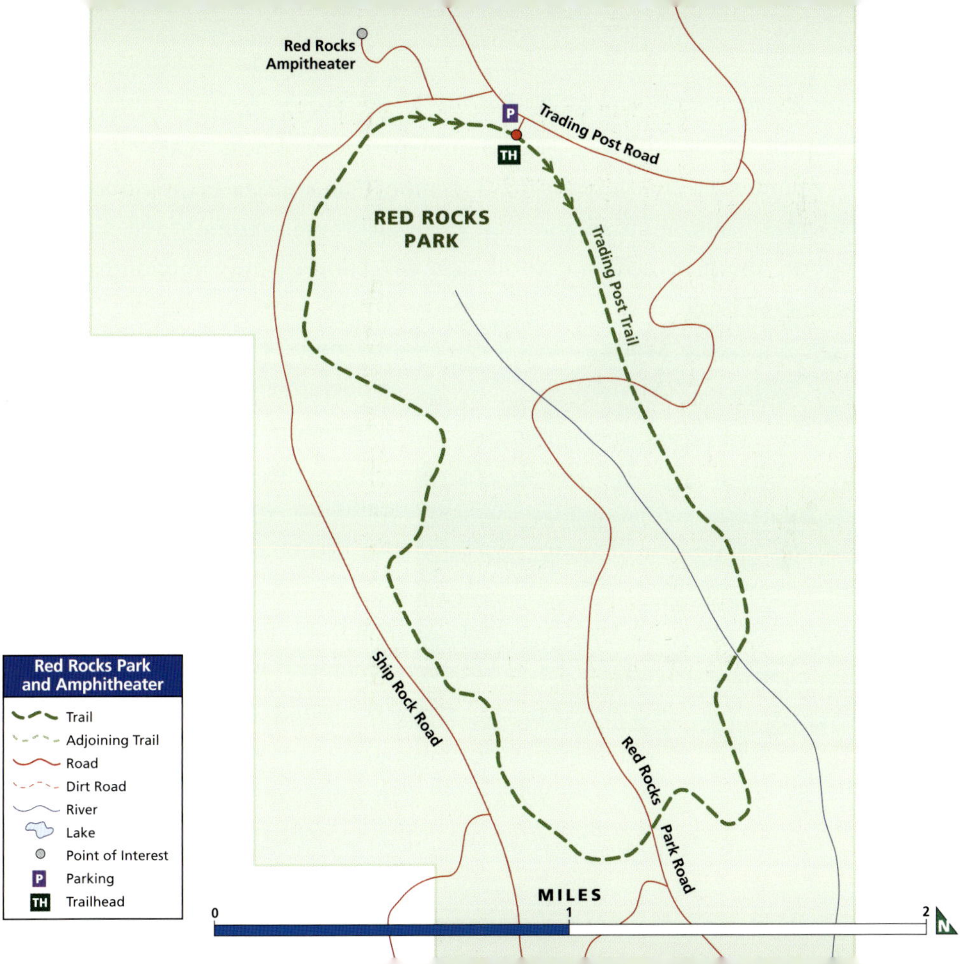
Red Rocks Ampitheater
Trading Post Road
TH
P
RED ROCKS PARK
Trading Post Trail
Ship Rock Road
Red Rocks Park Road
MILES
0
1
2
N
Red Rocks Park and Amphitheater
Trail
Adjoining Trail
Road
Dirt Road
River
Lake
Point of Interest
Parking
Trailhead

Famous for world-class entertainment, Red Rocks Park and Amphitheater, completed in 1941, is more than a spectacular outdoor venue reminiscent of an ancient Roman theater. Set in monumental red sandstone, the park boasts a world-class collection of huge monoliths.

Check out the chock-full trading post, which includes a bookstore featuring choice Colorado titles. The snack bar's outdoor balcony embraces an amazing red-rock view.

The scenic drive to access trailhead parking may be congested when an entertainment event is going on.

Park near the Trading Post. Begin the 1.4-mile **Trading Post Trail** loop at the southeast end of the parking lot. A map aims you down a few steps and turns you left. The trail winds past rock walls and skirts an arroyo. Stone stairs precede and follow a road crossing. The trail then eases, passing through dry, sloping, grassy meadows.

Within sight of the Dakota Hogback Formation, the route turns from south to west and crosses an arroyo via a sturdy footbridge. Curving around to head northwest near jutting red sandstone, the trail comes to a road crossing.

More intimate now, the track rises steadily, passing more massive, layered sculptures of 300 million-year-old sandstone. The next trail section winds gently up an old roadbed as it closely passes formations and wild plum thickets. Pass through a grassy bowl surrounded by more grandly eroded rock. Farther on, footbridges send the trail up a long series of rock steps in close proximity to a high Fountain Formation wall. Arrive at a road and turn right onto a narrow path that will return you to the Red Rocks Trading Post.

While You're There...

The steep walk up to the amazing Red Rocks Amphitheatre, originally known as the Garden of Angels, is an experience that shouldn't be missed. The view of Denver and the plains from this geologically formed, open-air theatre is more than memorable. Located between the dramatic 400-foot monoliths of Ship Rock and Creation Rock, the area has been attracting musical performers for the past century. Try the park's Ship Rock Grille for good food and ambiance.

South Valley Park

Swallow/Coyote Song

Distance	2.8-mile balloon loop
Difficulty	Easy
Elevation Gain	300 feet
Dogs	On leash
Directions	From Denver, travel south on CO 470. Exit westbound onto West Ken Caryl Ave., then turn left onto South Valley Rd. Parking is to your left.
Highlights	Red and yellow sandstone outcrops; picnic shelters; grasslands

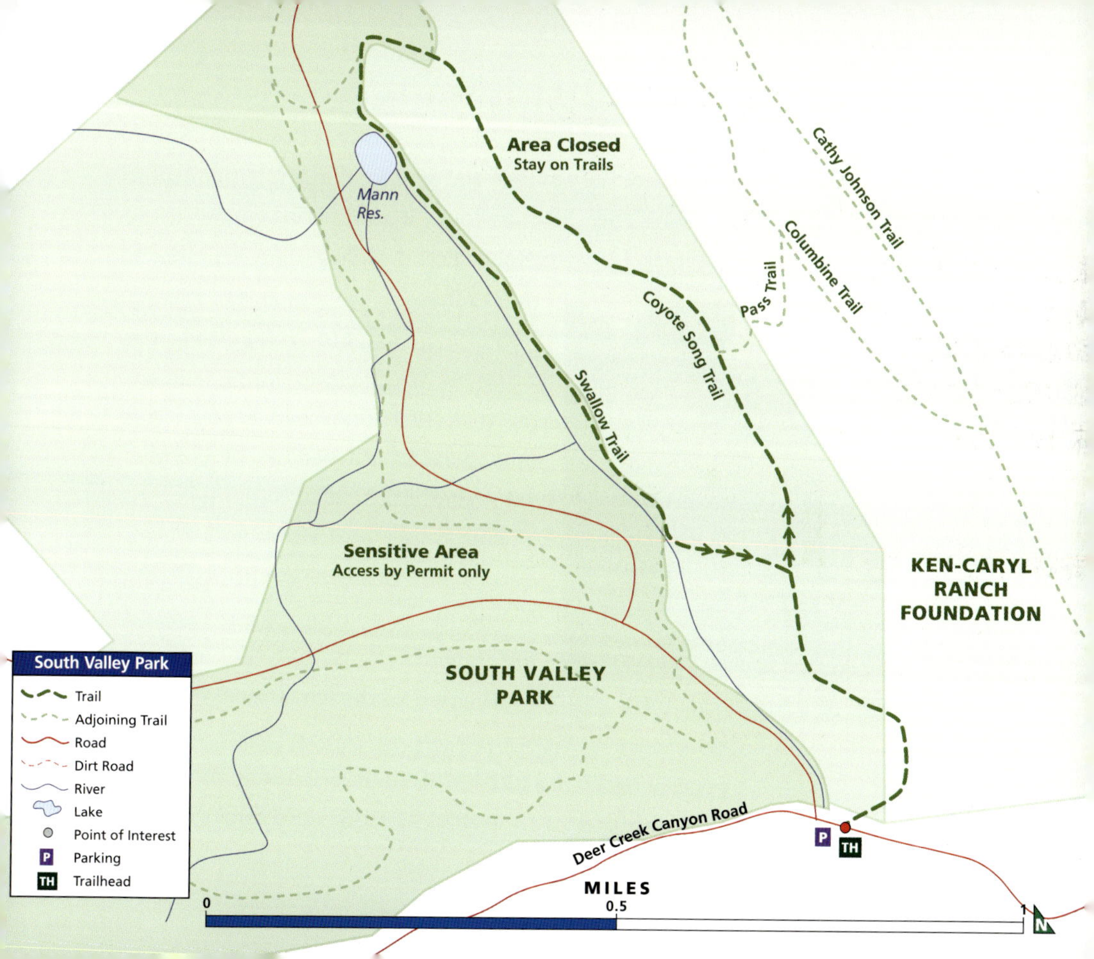
Area Closed
Stay on Trails
Mann Res.
Cathy Johnson Trail
Columbine Trail
Pass Trail
Coyote Song Trail
Swallow Trail
Sensitive Area
Access by Permit only
KEN-CARYL RANCH FOUNDATION
SOUTH VALLEY PARK
Deer Creek Canyon Road
P
TH
South Valley Park
Trail
Adjoining Trail
Road
Dirt Road
River
Lake
Point of Interest
Parking
Trailhead
MILES
0
0.5
1
N

Red sandstone outcrops and arching hogback ridges dominate South Valley Park Open Space. Grasslands and scrub oak complement these dramatic formations along this 2.8-mile loop. Parking is adequate in the lot adjacent to Deer Creek Canyon Road. Park brochures are available at the trailhead.

Start up **Coyote Song Trail,** the string of the balloon loop. Ancient red-rock formations lead to grasslands interspersed with patches of Gambel oak, commonly called scrub oak.

Follow the trail through a meadowy vale studded with jutting Fountain Formation sculptures. A fork arrives, beginning the balloon portion of the loop; you will return on the trail to the left. Bear right, and continue to enjoy the widening view.

Climb easily into scrublands fortified with a never-ending supply of colorful formations, including the pale wall of petrified sand dunes known as the Lyons Formation. The reds of the Fountain Formation's freestanding sculptures still dominate.

Passing the **Lyons Back Trail** on your right, continue north on Coyote Song and swoop into another grassy swale. A bike path starts off on your right. Shortly after, you'll come upon another junction. Turn left here, leaving Coyote Song Trail to join **Swallow Trail.** Bikes are not allowed on this section of the trail. Off to the right, picnic shelters and tables with marvelous views are sited. An alternate parking area and restrooms are also below.

> **Hike Smart**
>
> "30/30 Lightning Safety Rule: If the time between seeing a lightning flash and hearing the thunder is 30 seconds or less, seek shelter immediately."
>
> —Meteorologist Mike Nelson, author of the *Colorado Weather Almanac.*

Level and even underfoot, this cruising segment takes you south. Pass little Mann Reservoir. High up on a towering sandstone face to the left, mud nests of swallows cling, hence the trail's name.

Before a grove of cottonwoods and a few willows appears on the right, the far view displays ridges of various formations. Go left at the next intersection. When you reach the loop's "string," head right and retrace your steps back to your vehicle.

Waterton Canyon

Colorado Trail

Distance	8.0 miles roundtrip
Difficulty	Easy
Elevation Gain	100 feet
Dogs	Not permitted
Directions	From Denver, take I-25 south to CO 470. Head west for 12 miles on CO 470, then exit towards CO 121 S/Wadsworth Blvd. Take a left on Wadsworth Blvd. Go left on Waterton Canyon Rd. for 0.3 mile, then turn left into the fenced parking area.
Highlights	Bighorn sheep sighting opportunities; majestic canyon; river

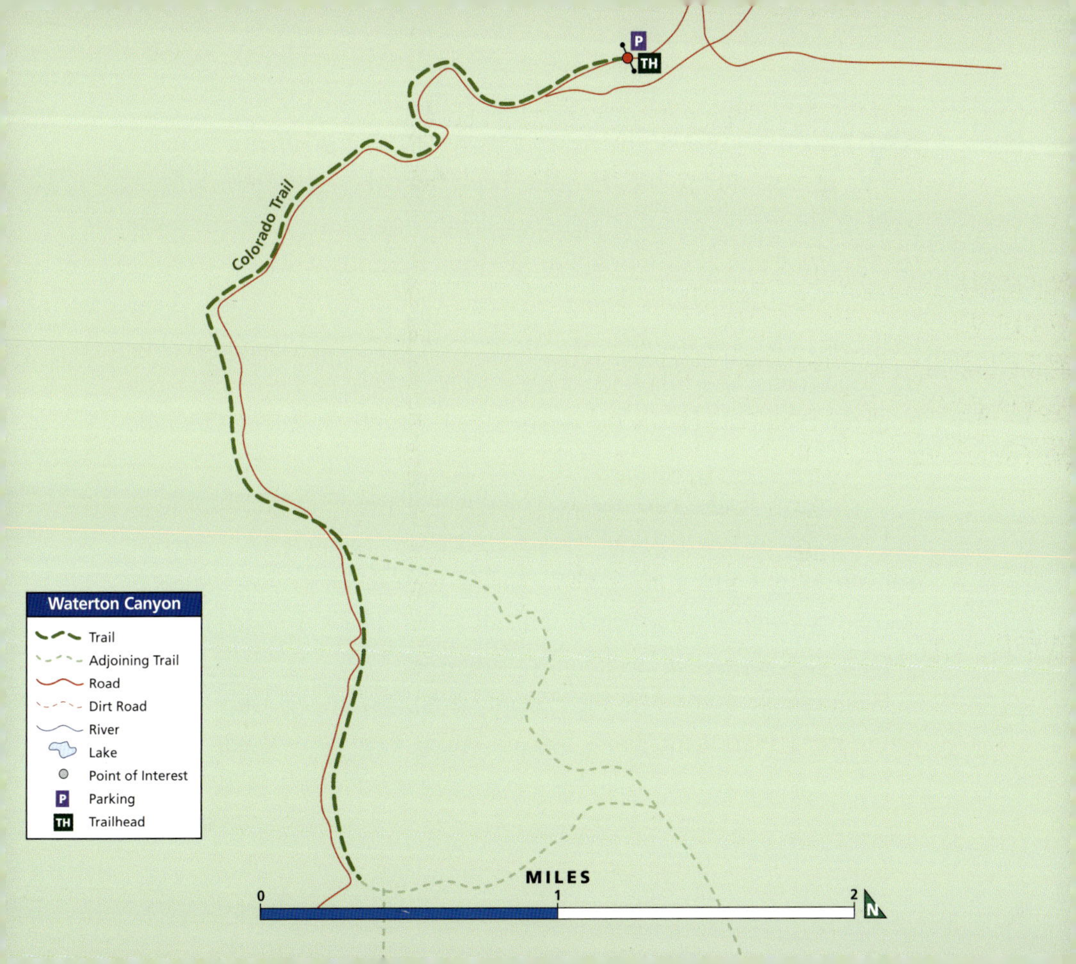
Colorado Trail
P
TH
Waterton Canyon
Trail
Adjoining Trail
Road
Dirt Road
River
Lake
Point of Interest
Parking
Trailhead
MILES
0
1
2
N

What other hike in the greater Denver-metro area offers the chance of not only seeing, but also being in rather close proximity to bighorn sheep? Be alert for bighorns clambering down from the rocky heights above you as they head for the clear South Platte River.

The road that this hike follows through heavily used Waterton Canyon eventually arrives at the great wall of Strontia Springs Dam. Bikers, hikers, equestrians, and fisherman share the big parking area across the road from the trailhead. This is the beginning of the 470-mile-long **Colorado Trail** as well.

Leaving the fenced parking area, head west across busy Waterton Road and proceed to the trailhead information board to study the Waterton Canyon Map. Cross a paved zone. Before the canyon begins, a mass of hoary cottonwoods shade scattered picnic tables. The wide road takes you towards the canyon-confined South Platte River.

Willows take over where the canyon starts. Pass under a pipeline just before the 1-mile mark. From here on you're in bighorn sheep habitat.

Carving its canyon ever deeper, the South Platte runs over a rocky bed as it turns a corner at a check dam where there are picnic tables and restrooms.

Willows guard the waterway as it passes a side canyon and a dip. Canyon walls fall back a bit to broaden the towering scene as a bend marks the 2.5-mile point. More picnic facilities and a restroom are located here.

Follow canyon contours to reach a sheet of lacy water flowing evenly down the slanted concrete face of Marston Diversion Dam. The 4-mile mark is reached along here and makes a good turnaround point.

Animal Alert!

As canyon heights increase, watch for bighorn sheep. These wild sheep live in herds and can climb steep mountainsides. Named for the large, curved horns that the males possess, bighorns can range in color from light to dark brown and sometimes gray, with a white rump and lining on the back of their legs. To spot them, look for the white coloring as they blend into the rocks.

Lair O' the Bear

Creekside/Bruin Bluff

Distance	2.0-mile loop
Difficulty	Easy
Elevation Gain	260 feet
Dogs	On leash
Directions	From Denver, take 1-70 west to CO 470 and head south. Head west on CO 74 and continue through the town of Morrison. Parking for Lair O' the Bear Open Space Park is about 4 miles ahead on the south side of the highway.
Highlights	Wide variety of habitats; creek-side picnic areas; fishing platform; wildflowers

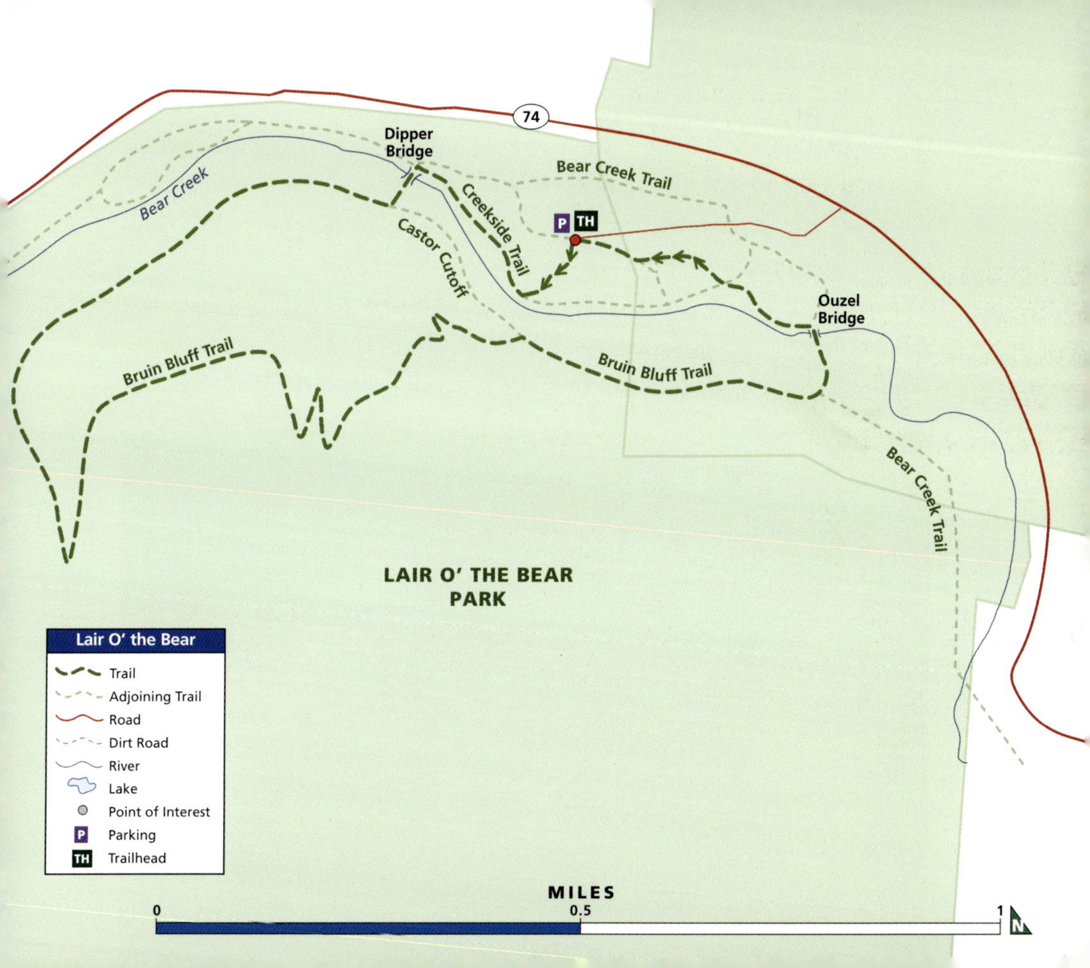

74
Dipper Bridge
Bear Creek Trail
Bear Creek
Creekside Trail
Castor Cutoff
P
TH
Ouzel Bridge
Bruin Bluff Trail
Bruin Bluff Trail
Bear Creek Trail
LAIR O' THE BEAR PARK
Lair O' the Bear
Trail
Adjoining Trail
Road
Dirt Road
River
Lake
Point of Interest
Parking
Trailhead
MILES
0
0.5
1
N

Lair O' the Bear, a close-in Jefferson County Open Space park, nestles in a canyon cut through by Bear Creek. The park's handicapped-accessible picnic facilities, fishing, hiking trails, and variety of wildflowers make it an excellent destination. Restrooms are available.

In its 2 miles, Bruin Bluff loop passes through a variety of habitats, ranging from riparian to dry scrubland, and from conifer forest to grassy slope. Parking is generous, but the popularity of Lair O' the Bear makes it

a busy place on weekends. Be alert for summer afternoon thunderstorms.

From the parking area, follow the **Creekside Trail** west to the Dipper bridge, named for the interesting bobbing behavior of the American dipper bird, also called the water ouzel.

After crossing the bridge, turn right (west). The trail climbs a rocky slope, then levels out along a north-facing exposure. Conifers appear and, in early spring, hundreds, perhaps thousands, of purple pasqueflowers bloom here. Benches are strategically placed along the trail.

Near the high point of the trail juts a rugged outcrop. The track switchbacks down—where it levels and reaches a junction with **Castor Cutoff,** stay right (east) on **Bruin Bluff Trail.**

Continue about 0.3 miles, then head left under cottonwoods, box elders, and willows to reach Ouzel Bridge—cross it, then aim left, passing some picnic sites. The restrooms mark the return route to the parking area. A hand-powered water pump offers cool refreshment. The park also offers picnic areas near the creek and a fishing platform that is popular with kids.

While You're There...

In the fall, Lair O' the Bear presents an entire slope of smooth sumac blazing forth in bright scarlet, attracting camera lenses and admirers. To get there, walk east from Ouzel Bridge on Bear Creek's south side.

Elk Meadows

Painters Pause/Founders/Meadow View

Distance	2.5-mile balloon loop
Difficulty	Easy
Elevation Gain	380 feet
Dogs	On leash
Directions	From Denver, take I-70 west to exit 252. Merge onto CO 74 E/Evergreen Parkway. Turn right at Lewis Ridge Rd. and continue to trailhead.
Highlights	Wetlands habitat; wildflowers; rugged outcrops

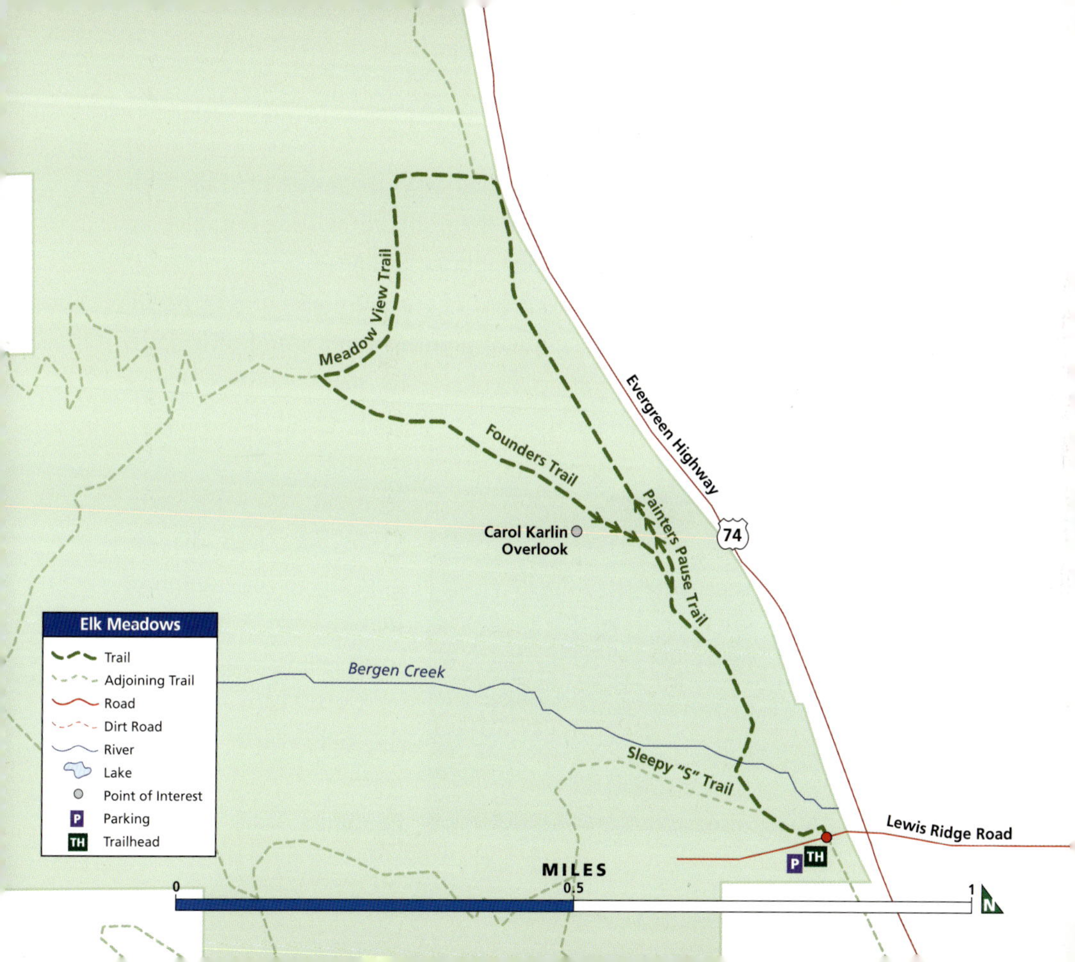

Meadow View Trail
Founders Trail
Painters Pause Trail
Evergreen Highway
74
Carol Karlin Overlook
Bergen Creek
Sleepy "S" Trail
Lewis Ridge Road
P
TH
Elk Meadows
Trail
Adjoining Trail
Road
Dirt Road
River
Lake
Point of Interest
Parking
Trailhead
MILES
0
0.5
1
N

Nearly 1,400 montane acres comprise Elk Meadows, a Jefferson County Open Space Park threaded with 13 miles of trail. This meadow-dominated loop covers 2.5 of them. Before starting out, pick up a trail map. Parking is generous at the popular trailhead.

Start out heading right on a raised bed of crusher fines—this is the tail end of **Sleepy "S" Trail.** Pass a family of ponderosa pines and drift down

to meet **Painters Pause Trail.** Head left (north), passing a wetlands area spangled with wildflowers. Wide skies lead the eye west, up to the summit of Bergen Peak. A boardwalk spans another damp zone.

A small barn appears on the right where the trail reaches a junction with **Founders Trail,** the path on which this loop will return. For now, stay right on Painters Pause. The route dips a bit, encountering another small wetlands spanned by a raised foot bed. Rise into the welcome shade of lonesome patriarch ponderosas.

Continue north—a view of Squaw Pass Road, which access Mount Evans, opens up. The next trail junction sends the loop left, on the **Meadow View Trail.** Drift gently up as the route turns southward. A ponderosa parkland underlain by granite outcrops sports an inviting bench. The loop soon meets another junction—turn left on Founders Trail. A broad hairpin bends the path out into the open meadow again.

Animal Alert!

Keep your eyes open for elk herds, especially when they drift into the far edges of the big meadow or congregate on the hillside north of the road. The first stretch of Squaw Pass Road, the alternate access route to Mount Evans, is good for viewing.

A half-circle offshoot leads to a pair of curved concrete benches and an interpretive sign honoring the legacy of Jefferson County Open Space. Guarded by a trio of noble ponderosas, a nearby plaque commemorates those who spearheaded efforts to acquire the many Jeffco open space parks. Soon after, the balloon portion of this route closes, rejoining the Painters Pause string, which leads back to the parking lot.

Meyer Ranch
Owl Perch/Lodge Pole

Distance 2.0-mile loop

Difficulty Easy

Elevation Gain 300 feet

Dogs On leash

Directions From Denver, go west on 6th Ave. Exit to 1-70 W. Merge with CO 470 E and continue 5.7 miles. Exit to US 285 S and continue 11 miles. Turn left onto S. Turkey Creek Rd. The Meyer Ranch Park Trailhead is on your immediate right.

Highlights Wildflowers; tuft-eared Abert's squirrel sighting opportunities

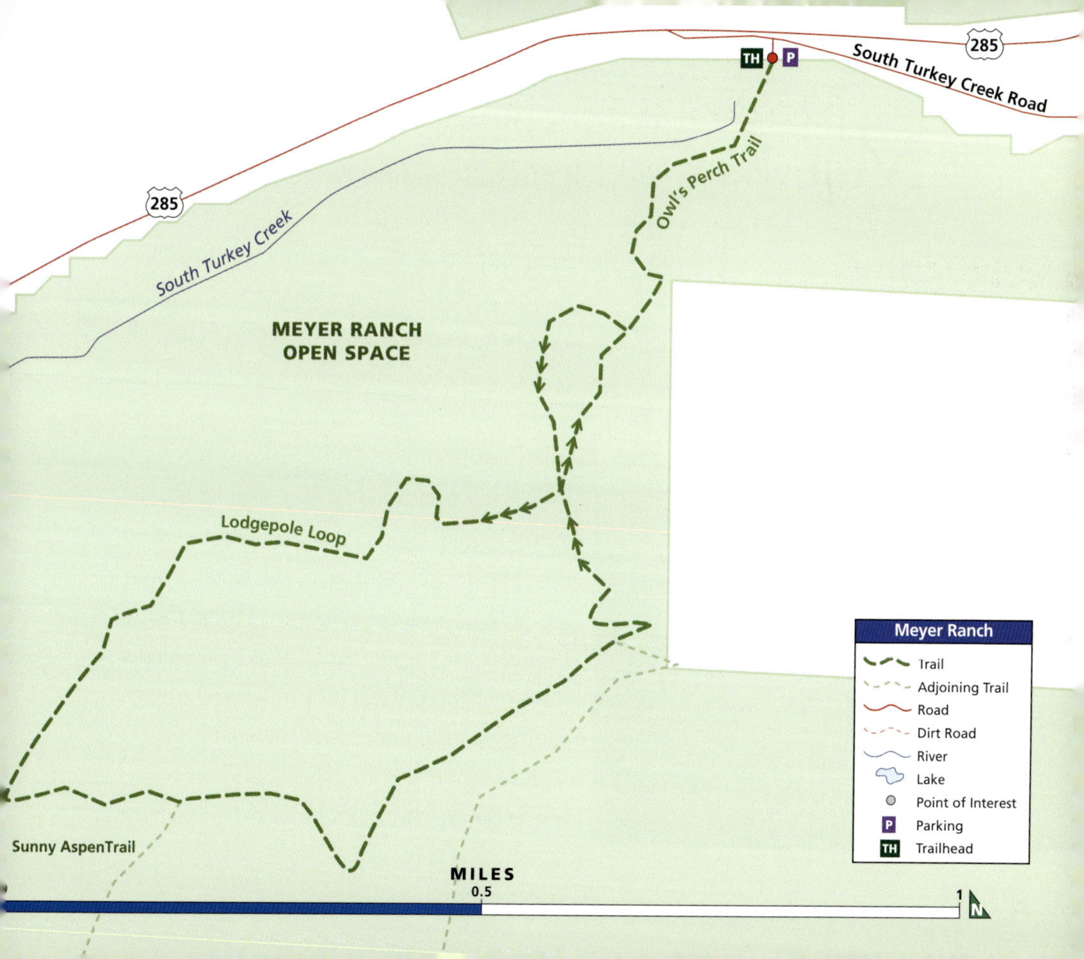
285
South Turkey Creek Road
TH
P
Owl's Perch Trail
285
South Turkey Creek
MEYER RANCH
OPEN SPACE
Lodgepole Loop
Sunny AspenTrail
MILES
0.5
1
N
Meyer Ranch
Trail
Adjoining Trail
Road
Dirt Road
River
Lake
Point of Interest
Parking
Trailhead

Meyer Ranch Open Space Park, situated in a beautiful valley, was once a working ranch and part-time ski hill. The lush front meadow of this Douglas County Open Space Park teems with wildflowers. Fenced trailhead parking—trail maps are available nearby—fills quickly on summer weekends. Arrive early for a spot.

Begin on the wildflower-flanked **Owl's Perch Trail.** South Turkey Creek flows through the plush meadow. The wide trail turns a corner, then rises gradually through a selection of native wildflowers, including dusky purple sugarbowls, waving white bistort, and Colorado blue columbine.

Where the trail divides near the restrooms, head right. At a second junction, the loop heads right again to reach a split log bench shaded by aspens. The pathway meanders up under good-sized ponderosa pines—favored habitat of tuft-eared Abert's squirrels, which are often charcoal black.

Pines give way to aspens, and a turn to the right at the next junction takes you onto **Lodgepole Loop,** where the sign simply states: "trail." The path levels and enters mixed conifers. A small drainage dappled by aspen shade leads to a slight rise, lifting the track to another level section.

A service road crosses the trail; stay to the right and continue on Lodgepole Loop. A bit farther along, a switchback draws the route up to an area studded with old stumps. About a mile into the hike, a junction sends **Sunny Aspen Trail** off to the right; continue straight on Lodgepole Loop. The trail flattens along here, leading down over a culvert-bridged drainage, then into a sunny little meadow featuring perfumed wild roses.

Lodge Pole Loop heads left at intersection with Sunny Aspen Trail, then descends via easy-going switchbacks. Turn right to join the eastern segment of the Owl Perch Trail, which cruises down the east side of the picnic area. Return through the flowery meadow to reach the parking area.

Fun Fact

This area has an exciting and rich history important to Colorado. It is named for its former owners Norman and Ethel Meyers. Legend has it that the P.T. Barnum Circus used the ranch to house animals in the winters of the late 1880s. When Norman Meyer was remodeling the house in 1995 he found a board with the inscription, "Circus Town, 1889." Additionally, part of what is now Meyer Ranch was used as a ski hill in the 1940s. Remnants are still visible in the upper area of the park.

Roxborough State Park

Fountain Valley Loop

Distance 2.25-mile loop, plus spur

Difficulty Easy

Elevation Gain 250 feet

Dogs Not permitted

Directions From Denver, take I-25 west to CO 470 east. Exit onto CO 121/South Wadsworth Blvd. Turn left onto Waterton Rd., then right onto North Rampart Range Rd. Turn left at North Roxborough Park Rd., then right onto Roxborough Dr.

Fees & Info Yearly Colorado State Parks Pass $60; day pass $6. For more information, call (303) 973-3959.

Highlights Meadows of wildflowers; dramatic rock formations; wildlife spotting opportunities; historic stone house; try the moonlight hike, which includes a dessert buffet

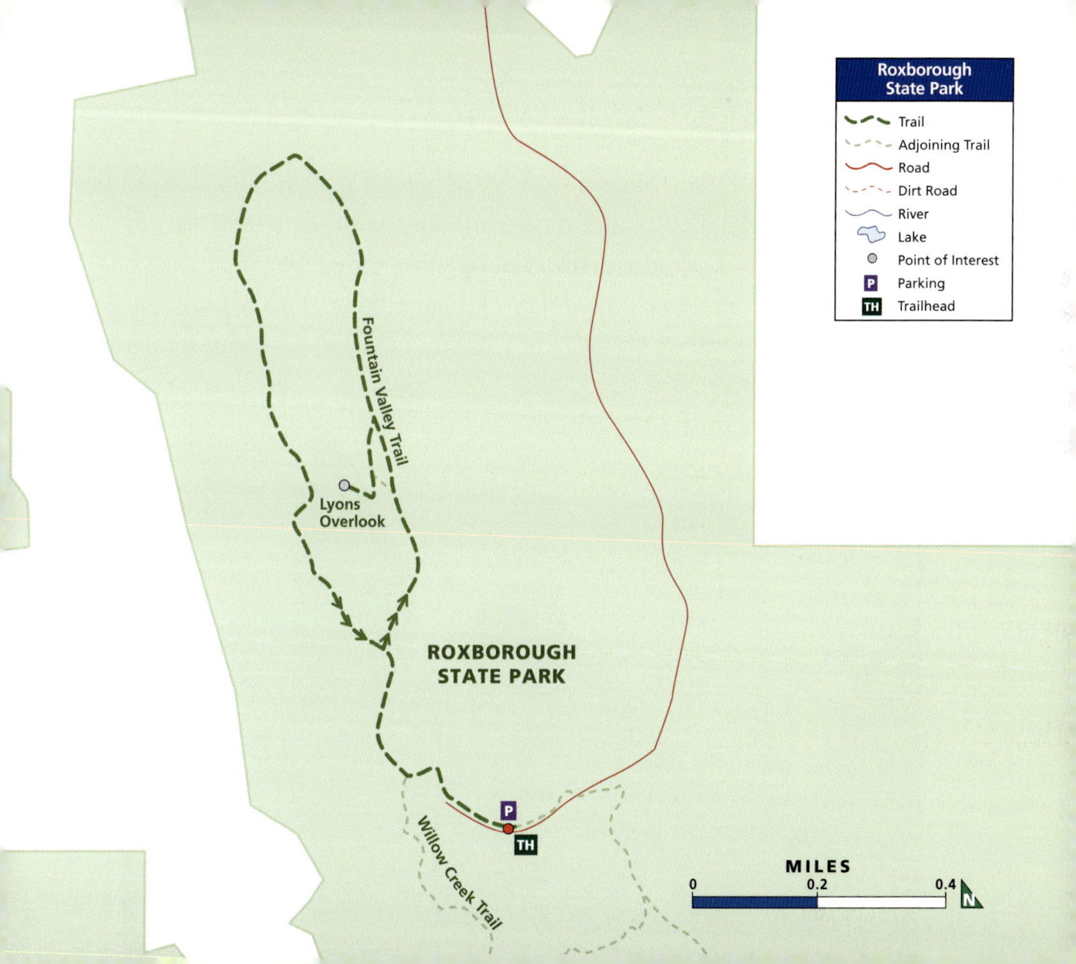

Roxborough State Park
Trail
Adjoining Trail
Road
Dirt Road
River
Lake
Point of Interest
Parking
Trailhead
Fountain Valley Trail
Lyons Overlook
ROXBOROUGH STATE PARK
P
TH
Willow Creek Trail
MILES
0
0.2
0.4
N

The 2.25-mile Fountain Valley Loop bids you to discover a beautiful and peaceful place. Since no pets are permitted along this hikers-only trail, there exists a good chance to spot wildlife, particularly mule deer in early morning and late afternoon. Among other things, you'll pass wildflower-spattered meadows, a century-old stone house with a porch on which to ponder, and several rock formations, including the commanding Fountain Formation.

For a romantic excursion, experience this Roxborough State Park trail by moonlight. From late spring to autumn, you can, for a modest cost, reserve a spot on a naturalist-led full-moon hike. Just as enticing is the yummy dessert buffet spread out for moonlight hike participants in the visitors center.

Animal Alert!

Early spring is courtship time for dime-sized chorus frogs. They reside in a hidden pond where Fountain Valley Trail intersects Little Willow Creek at the frog-engraved post. Pause silently to hear their courting song.

Begin the **Fountain Valley Trail** from the flagstone visitors center patio and head right, on a natural surface road. Soon, a short spur on the left leads to a couple of benches prime for scenic contemplation. Back on the main trail, bear right at a fork where open meadows lead to the **Lyons Overlook spur.** Ascend to an observation deck surrounded by ponderosa pines, then return to the Fountain Valley Trail.

Continue down to the restored Persse Place, an ochre stone house built around 1900; the front porch makes a good place to sit and wonder what life might have been like here a hundred years ago. Meadows and soaring red sandstone formations grace the rest of the loop. Cross tiny Willow Creek and continue to hike, cradled between the Lyons Formation wall and the Fountain Formation fins. You'll eventually return to the visitors center.

Alderfer/Three Sisters Park

The Brother Loop

Distance	2.7-mile loop
Difficulty	Easy to moderate
Elevation Gain	400 feet
Dogs	Must be on leash.
Directions	From Denver, head west on I-70. Take exit 252 to merge onto CO 74 E/ Evergreen Parkway. In Evergreen, take a slight right on CO 73. Take another right onto Buffalo Park Rd. and continue 1.5 miles to the trailhead on your right.
Highlights	Metamorphic outcrops; panoramic views; peaceful, quiet area; wildflowers

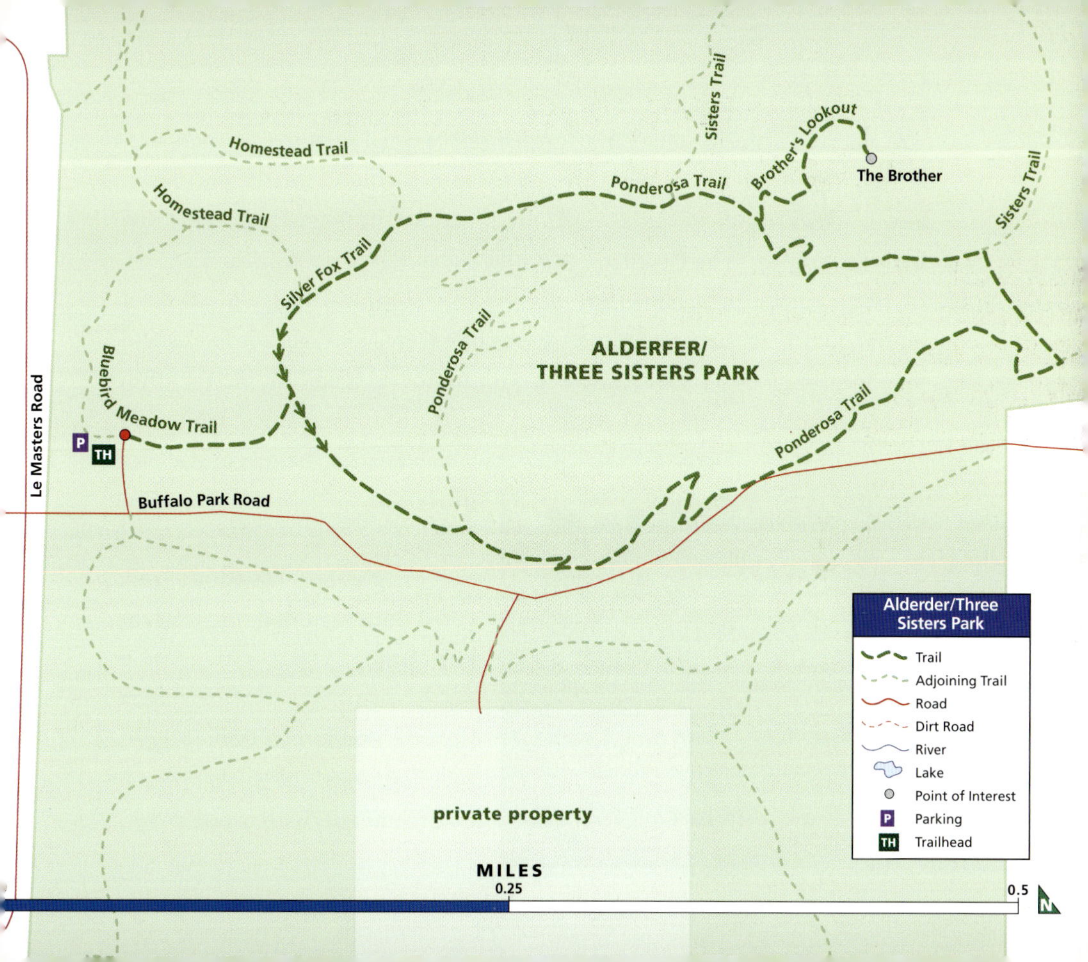

Homestead Trail
Homestead Trail
Sisters Trail
Brother's Lookout
The Brother
Ponderosa Trail
Sisters Trail
Silver Fox Trail
Ponderosa Trail
ALDERFER/
THREE SISTERS PARK
Bluebird Meadow Trail
Le Masters Road
P
TH
Buffalo Park Road
Ponderosa Trail
private property
Alderder/Three Sisters Park
Trail
Adjoining Trail
Road
Dirt Road
River
Lake
Point of Interest
Parking
Trailhead
MILES
0.25
0.5
N

Alderfer/Three Sisters Park, located just west of Evergreen, offers various trails that meander through meadows, conifer forests, and aspen groves. Rock outcrops and wildflowers accent the landscape along the trails leading to "The Brother," this hike's goal.

The Brother is a metamorphic outcrop composed largely of silver plume quartz. Its summit features views of 14,265-foot Mount Evans and is an ideal spot for a picnic. Spread a quilt on the rock and lift plastic flutes of your favorite beverage. A wedge of cheese, summer sausage, fruit, and a baguette fill the rest of the picnic bill.

From the parking lot, head east on **Bluebird Meadow Trail;** you'll soon turn right onto **Silver Fox Trail.** In 0.2 mile, you'll reach another juncture. Stay right on **Ponderosa Trail.** Rugged rock outcrops of silver plume quartz mingle with stout pines,

Douglas fir, and slender aspens. Ponderosa Trail wanders easily beneath namesake pines.

Imposing boulders announce a left turn onto **Sisters Trail;** after 0.1 mile, head left to rejoin Ponderosa Trail. Head right on the spur trail for The Brother. If you're a runner, you might choose to walk over the rough terrain that climbs to a broad summit, or skip the spur to The Brother altogether. From the summit, look due north to see the "Three Sisters." Head to the west side of the humped stone summit for an encompassing view of fourteener Mount Evans, particularly attractive when snowcapped.

Trail Etiquette

- Be courteous and keep noise to a minimum.
- Allow sufficient room for those wanting to pass.
- When passing other hikers from behind, announce your presence so as not to frighten your fellow trail users.
- Those coming downhill have the right of way.
- Always yield to equestrians.

Return down the rocky spur and turn right to continue the loop. Keep left at an intersection; at the next one, keep right to join **Silver Fox Trail.** Stay left at the next two intersections. Conifer shade gives way to more open ponderosa pine parkland. You'll leave Silver Fox Trail at the next intersection, turning right to rejoin Bluebird Meadow Trail and retrace your steps back to the parking lot.

Golden Gate Canyon State Park Burro/Mountain Lion

Distance	2.4 miles
Difficulty	Easy to moderate
Elevation Gain	400 feet
Dogs	Not permitted
Directions	From Denver, head west on US 6/6th Ave. Continue on CO 93. Just past Golden, take a left onto Golden Gate Canyon Rd. Continue for 14 miles. At the Golden Gate Canyon State Park visitors center, head right on Crawford Gulch Rd. and go 2.5 miles. Park at the Bridge Creek Trailhead.
Fees & Info	Fees and Information: Yearly Colorado State Parks Pass $60; day pass $6. For more information, call (303) 973-3959.
Highlights	Old homestead cabin; lush, blossoming meadows; serene pond and musical stream

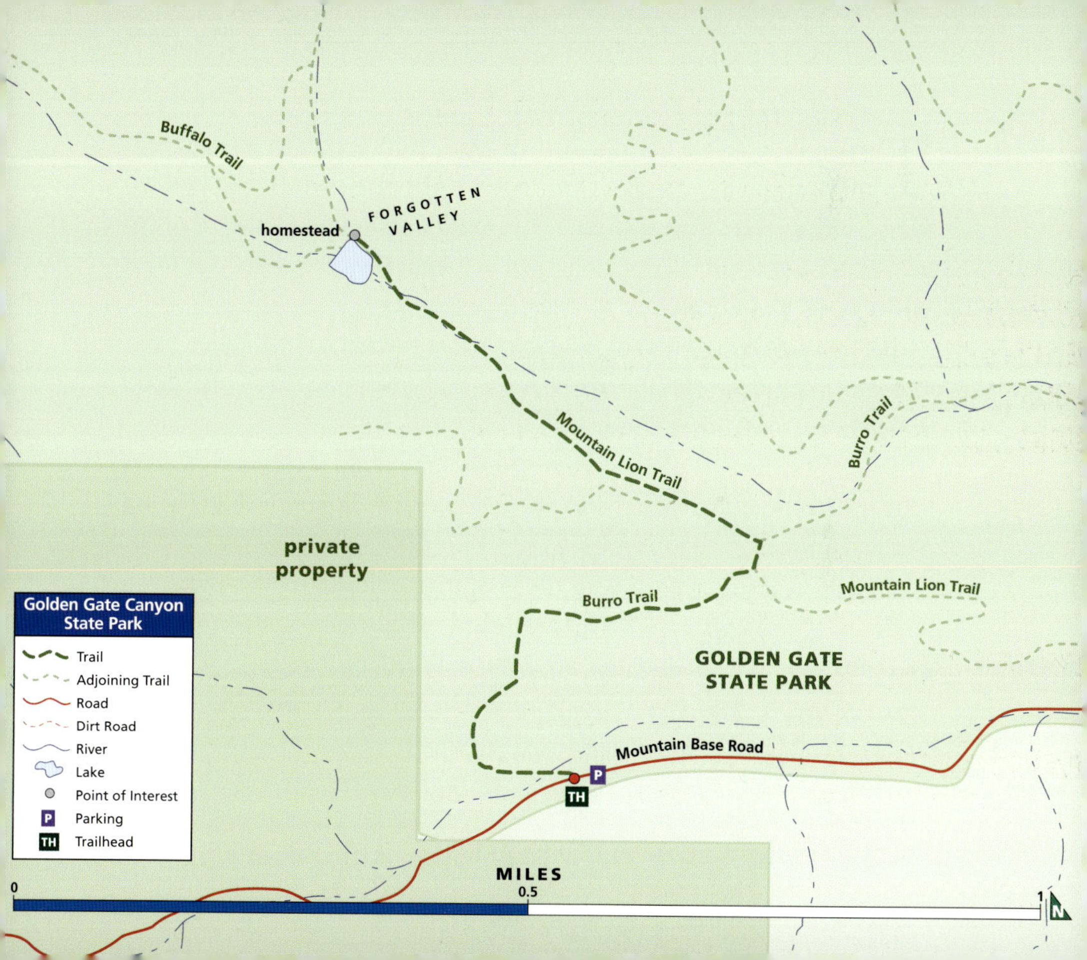
Buffalo Trail
FORGOTTEN VALLEY
homestead
Mountain Lion Trail
Burro Trail
private property
Burro Trail
Mountain Lion Trail
GOLDEN GATE STATE PARK
Mountain Base Road
P
TH
Golden Gate Canyon State Park
Trail
Adjoining Trail
Road
Dirt Road
River
Lake
Point of Interest
Parking
Trailhead
MILES
0
0.5
1
N

Twelve-thousand acres of varied habitats, fishing ponds, picnic areas, and campsites, as well as an impressive trail system, make Golden Gate Canyon State Park inviting. This route to Forgotten Valley leads to an 1870s homestead overlooking a serene pond; the cabin bids you to sit on its porch and dream.

Before embarking on your hike, stop in at the attractive Golden Gate Canyon State Park visitors center for a trail brochure. Stroll the deck, which overlooks a trout pond.

Parking, shared by picnickers, is spread out among several paved areas near the trailhead. Arrive early for a spot—and to avoid summer afternoon thunderstorms.

The Burro Trail, marked with the hoofprint of its namesake, takes you under ponderosa pines to a map signboard, then over a bridge spanning Ralston Creek. The trail swings left along the stream where a sign indicates that you are on your way to Forgotten Valley. The trail becomes steeper and rockier where it enters ponderosa parkland.

A junction sends the route to Forgotten Valley left, along **Mountain Lion Trail.** Lodgepole pines aim the wide, gentle track down by aspens, where running water chortles. After crossing a little creek, the track pulls up to an old dam face, and the valley named Forgotten unfolds to reveal a serene pond—look for the old homestead cabin on the far shore. Occupied by the Swedish Tallman family until the 1950s, it is now listed on the Colorado State Register of Historic Places.

To reach the restored cabin's front porch, walk on the road past the dam, then turn left to dip into a flowery meadow and seep. The covered porch is the perfect place to enjoy snacks and daydreams before returning the way you came, your steps lighter and brighter from your visit to Forgotten Valley.

Why Not...

Experiencing a bit of the historic West as seen at Forgotten Valley's 1870s homestead might be enhanced by a book of Victorian poetry. Bring cookies and lemonade to enjoy on the shady porch.

Peak 8 Colorado SuperChair Nature Walk

Distance 2.0 miles

Difficulty Easy to moderate

Elevation Gain 381 feet

Dogs Not permitted on chairlift

Directions From Denver, take I-70 west to exit 203/Frisco. Head south on CO 9 and follow signs to Breckenridge Ski Resort Peak 8 parking lot. Take the Colorado SuperChair.

Fees & Info Chairlift fee required. Call (970) 453-5000 for more information.

Highlights Fun and exciting chairlift ride; sweeping mountain views; wildflowers

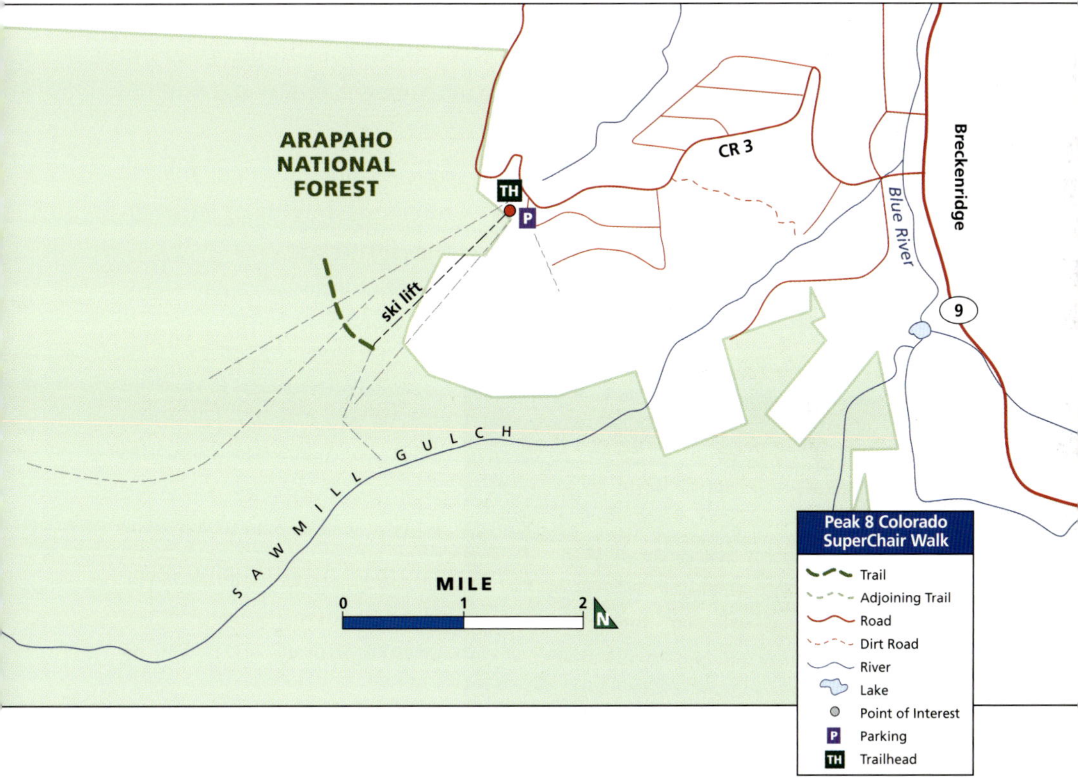
ARAPAHO
NATIONAL
FOREST
TH
P
ski lift
CR 3
Breckenridge
Blue River
9
SAWMILL GULCH
MILE
0
1
2
N
Peak 8 Colorado SuperChair Walk
Trail
Adjoining Trail
Road
Dirt Road
River
Lake
Point of Interest
Parking
Trailhead

A fun and effortless way to ascend over 1,000 vertical feet to immerse your soul in high-country wildflowers is offered at Breckenridge Ski Area. Not only is riding the Peak 8 Colorado SuperChair fast and fun, the return trip offers stunning mountain panoramas.

The trail begins at a wetlands glade and continues through hillside meadows so flowery one wishes for a book of poetry. Trail maps are available when you purchase a modestly priced chairlift ticket.

One caveat: when thunderstorms hit, the chairlift closes down until lightning is no longer within 12 miles. Plan to take the chairlift's first morning run to avoid summer afternoon thunderstorms. Additionally, keep track of time to catch the last chairlift down—it is a long hike back to the base. Summer parking is free and plentiful in the Peak 8 lots.

At the Peak 8 Colorado SuperChair offload point, the chair slows to a crawl. Unload and walk off a few yards to a map indicating that the Nature Trail begins to the right. Further signage explains elevation-influenced ecosystems, such as tundra, which typically begins around 11,500 feet in this part of the Rockies. Spruce flanks the trail as it winds up past another interpretive sign.

The trail, garlanded by flowers, ascends to a bowl meadow. Continue on, to where krummholz (meaning crooked wood in German) islands and boulders anchor the trail. The distant Continental Divide lifts the eastern horizon with Grays and Torreys Peaks, both fourteeners.

Climb up through spruce to where the trail opens onto a steep bank cloaked with a shattered rainbow of wildflowers. The trail weaves around rocks and trees, eventually coming to a T-bar lift. This is a good place to turn around.

Fun Fact

Breckenridge's Imperial Express SuperChair is the highest ski lift in all of North America. It was built in 2005 and is 12,840 feet above sea level. The lift is a two and a half minute ride compared to the alternative 45-minute hike up the mountain. Depending on the number of chairs it is running at the time, the SuperChair can carry as many as 1,800 riders up to the summit in one hour.

Matthews/Winter Park

Red Rocks/Morrison Slide

Distance	4.2-mile balloon loop
Difficulty	Easy to moderate
Elevation Gain	530 feet
Dogs	On leash
Directions	From Denver, take I-70 west to exit 259. Head south on County Road 93 under I-70. Take your first right onto Matthews/Winter Park access road. The trailhead is just past the footbridge.
Highlights	Wildflowers; ancient rock formations; creek

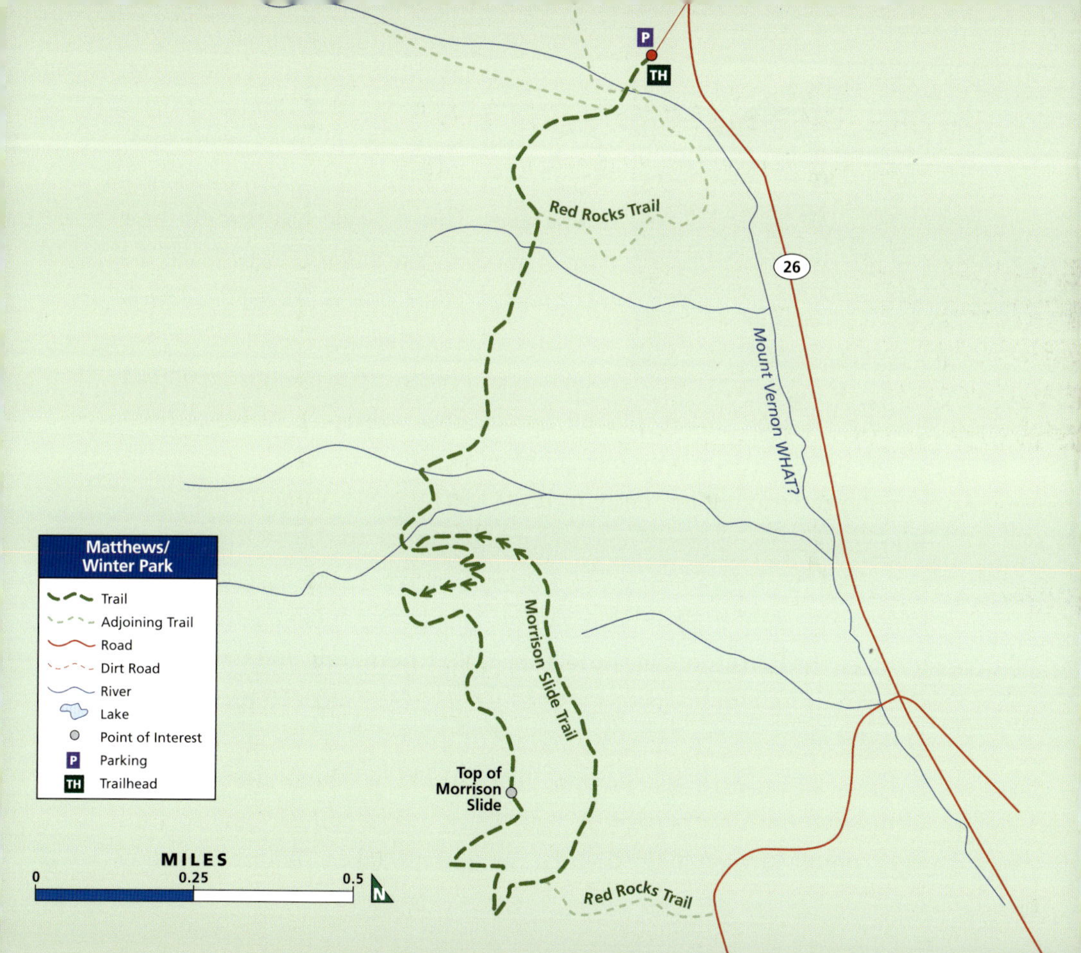

Matthews/
Winter Park
Trail
Adjoining Trail
Road
Dirt Road
River
Lake
Point of Interest
Parking
Trailhead
P
TH
Red Rocks Trail
26
Mount Vernon WHAT?
Morrison Slide Trail
Top of
Morrison
Slide
Red Rocks Trail
MILES
0
0.25
0.5
N

Convenient to the Denver metro area, Matthews/Winter Park encompasses over 1,100 acres. This 4.2-mile hike affords great views—watch for the Dakota Hogback and the red sandstone Fountain Formation. Wildflowers are spattered throughout the loop.

Mountain bikers share the busy trailhead parking lot, which often fills on fine weather weekends. Arrive early to secure a spot. Pick up a park map before starting your hike.

From the parking lot, ease down to clear little Mt. Vernon Creek and, after crossing the footbridge, travel straight ahead and curve south along rising Red Rocks Trail. At a "T" intersection, where the spur to the Mt. Vernon cemetery heads west, continue south. Dip briefly into a small, brush-choked ravine along the leveling trail. Contouring and undulating, the trail drifts into an arroyo shaded by box elder trees to meet a lone Douglas fir.

Rise slightly, passing outcrops, then cautiously s-curve down a loose segment to cross a drainage. A switchback ascent prepares you to turn right, onto Morrison Slide Trail. Easing upward, take a moment to study the Dakota Hogback ridge to the east—a locally renowned repository for dinosaur-era evidence. Switchback on the steadily ascending trail to enter a section of tumbled red sandstone boulders.

Zigzag up on rockier footing to where the trail bisects an area of big boulders and reach an escarpment's flat bench, taking in a far-reaching panorama that features Green Mountain in the foreground. Wend toward the bench's far side and drop via rugged switchbacks. Junipers stud the landscape clear to the Red Rocks Amphitheater.

While You're There...

The Dakota Hogback formation seen to the east has fine examples of three-toed dinosaur prints on its east side, adjacent to Alameda Parkway. Periodically, the road is closed to traffic and docents teach visitors about the formation's dinosaur connection. There is also a great visitors center at the base of Dinosaur Ridge that has lots of cool dinosaur stuff. (303) 697-3466.

Watch your footing on the uneven path as it quickly descends. A signed junction continues the loop slightly left and up a short incline. Farther on, as the route heads north, trailsides harbor patches of glossy-leaved poison ivy: "leaves of three, leave them be . . ."

Cruise along the escarpment's foot, heading back towards the creek drainage to complete the balloon portion of the loop; only the string remains. At the rail fence triangle, stay left to travel down to a zigzag and descend gently to the creek.

Green Mountain

Hayden Loop

Distance	3.0-mile loop
Difficulty	Moderate
Elevation Gain	690 feet
Dogs	On leash
Directions	From Denver, take 6th Ave./US 6 west to Union Blvd. Go left on Union Blvd., then right at W Alameda Parkway. Park at east trailhead across from Florida Dr.
Highlights	Summer wildflowers; views of five of Colorado's famed fourteeners

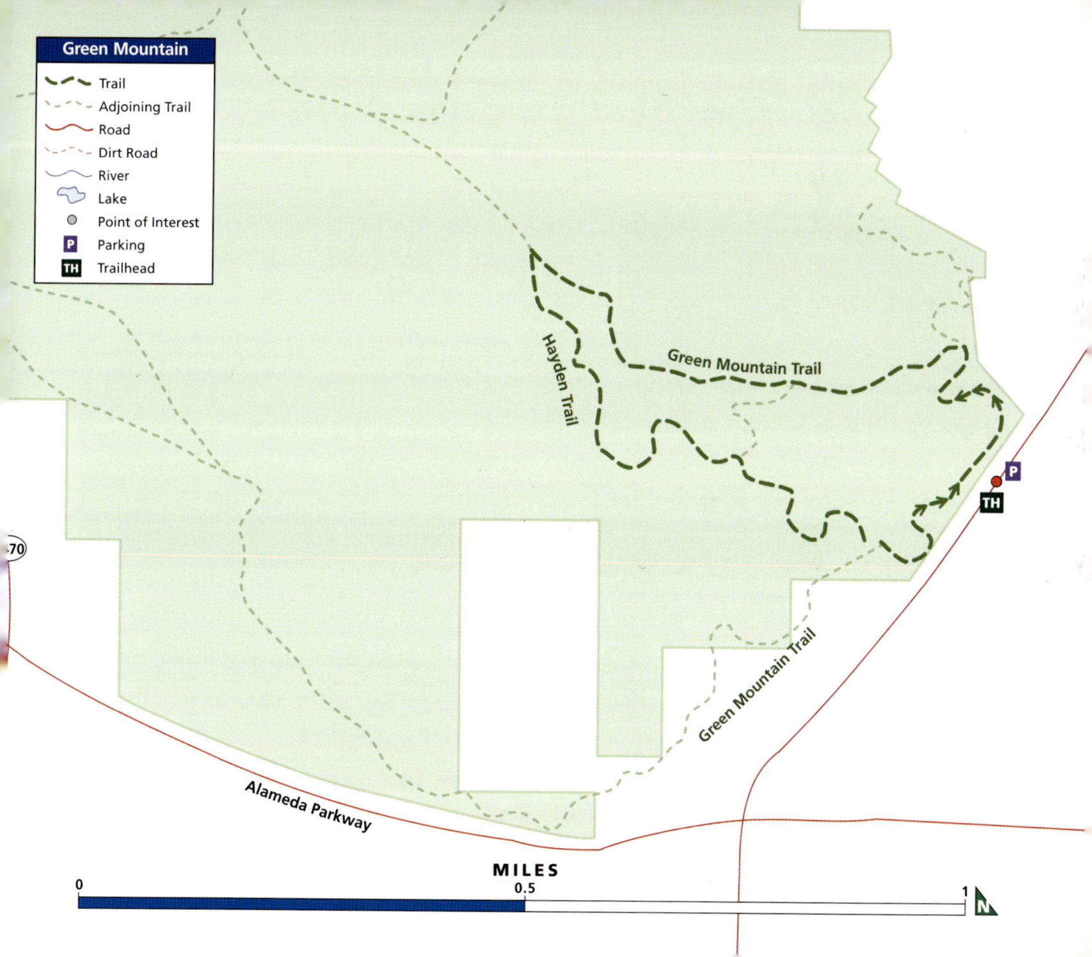
Green Mountain
Trail
Adjoining Trail
Road
Dirt Road
River
Lake
Point of Interest
Parking
Trailhead
P
TH
Green Mountain Trail
Hayden Trail
Green Mountain Trail
Alameda Parkway
70
MILES
0
0.5
1
N

On the western outskirts of Lakewood, a western suburb of Denver, Green Mountain rises like a gentle island in a sea of civilization. This "island" is wildflower happy, especially from late May to late June. While Green Mountain is long on seasonal color, it is short on shade, making early morning or evening hikes ideal. From the top, there is a 360-degree view of Denver, the Dakota Hogback, and a fourteener or two.

The City of Lakewood has done itself proud by keeping a whole mountain in its midst available to hikers, bikers, and horse riders. Much of the land was donated or sold to the city by the Hayden family, hence the name of the area: William Frederick Hayden Park. The large east-side parking area, shared by mountain bikers, maintains a sign indicating the beginning of the Hayden Trail. Pick up a handy trail map before starting off. Be alert for rattlesnakes and summer-afternoon thunderstorms.

The **Hayden Trail** leaves from the far end of the parking area and climbs an old jeep road, passing wildflower-studded cutbanks. Pause now and then to catch views of the cityscape that fans out eastward in a half circle.

Stay left at the first intersection; at the next one, stay right.

The trail rises quickly toward a radio tower. Farther on, as the trail crests, a short spur on the left leads to views of an arc of mountains which includes fourteeners Pike's Peak, Mount Evans, Grays Peak, Torreys Peak, and Longs Peak.

Continue north a bit on the main trail, which merges with a road. Take a very sharp left turn onto a well-defined trail that angles back towards the direction you came. Mount Evans can be seen on the western skyline. This junction begins the downhill leg of the loop and introduces a wealth of wildflowers. Later, Pikes Peak can be seen off to the south.

Animal Alert!

Be on the lookout for the non-venomous bull snake. Where rattlesnakes make their home, bull snakes usually move about. Fangless bull snakes have been known to shake their rattleless tails, emulating rattlers. Bull snakes can be found throughout the central United States—as far north as Canada and as far south as Mexico. They are usually larger than 6 feet in length and are commonly a yellowish color with brown, black, or red blotches.

Descend leisurely through waving grasses, and pass small ravines thick with chokecherry and hawthorn. Stay right at an intersection. At the next junction, keep left. Wind down southward, then bear east and finally north up a short incline paralleling Alameda Parkway. You'll soon be back at the parking area.

St. Louis Lake

Distance 7.0 miles out and back

Difficulty Moderate

Elevation Gain 1,531 feet

Dogs On leash

Directions Take US 40 north to Fraser. Take a left turn at the stoplight next to Safeway on County Road 72. Turn right immediately after the railroad underpass and then left on County Road 73/Forest Road 160. Continue for approximately 13 miles to the trailhead located at the end of the road.

Highlights Lively St. Louis Creek; wildflower-cloaked meadows; scenic lake

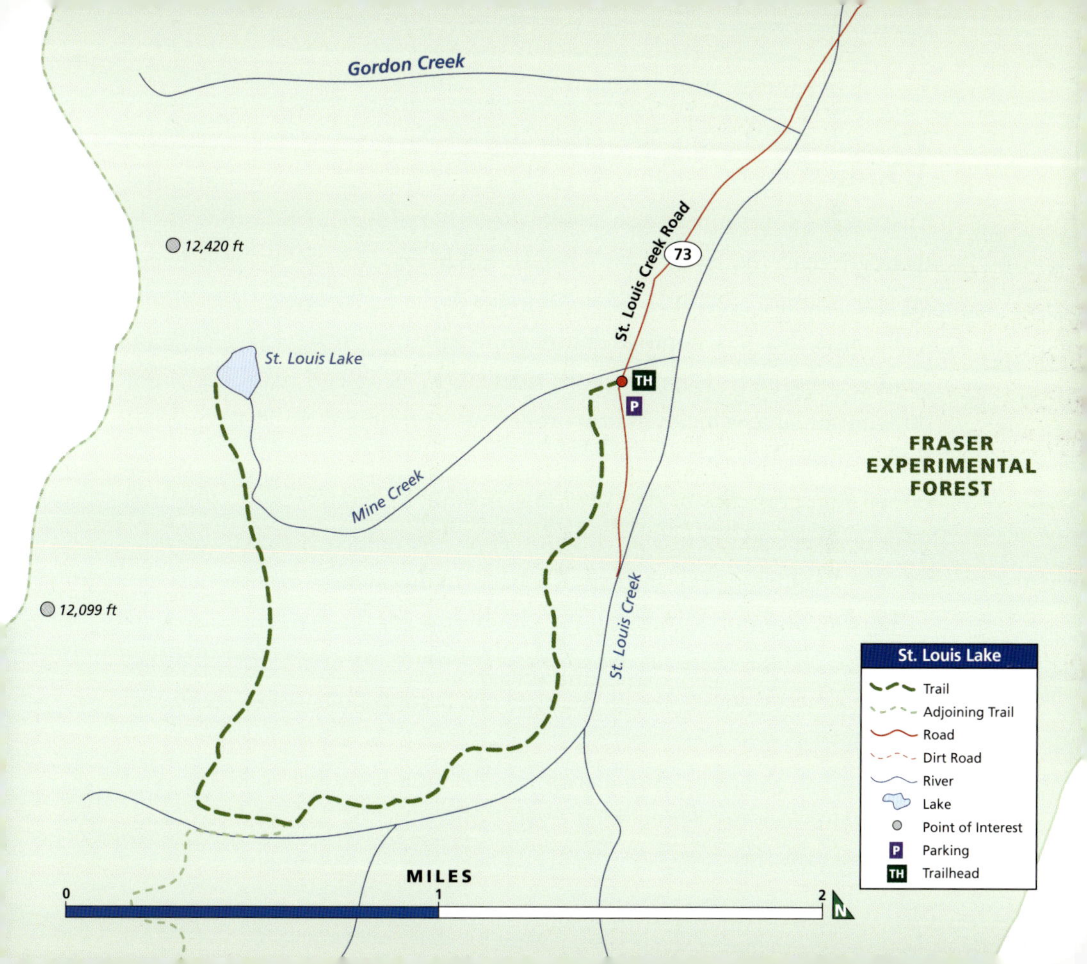

Gordon Creek
12,420 ft
St. Louis Creek Road
73
St. Louis Lake
TH
P
FRASER EXPERIMENTAL FOREST
Mine Creek
12,099 ft
St. Louis Creek
St. Louis Lake
Trail
Adjoining Trail
Road
Dirt Road
River
Lake
Point of Interest
Parking
Trailhead
MILES
0
1
2
N

Beguiling St. Louis Lake straddles the subalpine and alpine zones. Not only do the lake and it's flower-bedecked inlet offer a rewarding destination for adventurous hikers, but the string of meadows leading up to them are calico quilts of color when in full-bloom. Lively St. Louis Creek provides musical accompaniment for much of the 1,500-vertical-foot climb.

Because this is a popular destination, parking can be a challenge on summer weekends. Cars line both sides of the dead-end road, making it difficult for large vehicles to turn around at the trailhead. Be alert for afternoon thunderstorms.

Set out across the bridge spanning rushing St. Louis Creek. The trail pulls up over rocks before leveling for a bit. The trail and creek travel side-by-side, winding gently through the lush environment.

Leaving St. Louis Creek behind, climb through the depths of a spruce-fir forest. Where there are trees, there are roots, so watch your footing. Passing flowery pocket meadows, the trail becomes increasing rocky and uneven.

Return to the creek. You'll soon cross it on a hefty log. Take care and watch your footing. The golden creek courses openly, and the trail heads back up into big conifers. Emerge into a spectacular meadow. Every color imaginable covers several acres here during peak bloom in July.

The trail to St. Louis Peak branches off to your left—stay right. You'll see the peaks' treeless 12,246-foot summit from the next meadow. Ascend switchbacks, then pass through another meadow, crossing a little creeklet on a log bridge. Craggy outcrops rear into view.

The trail descends for a bit, and convenient stones help you cross a brook. Drier ground ahead takes the trail up a steep, brief pitch to more even terrain. Rugged mountains and a myriad of wildflowers make diverting company during the last pitch to reach St. Louis Lake. Backed by sky-sweeping crests, the jeweled waters dance in the summer sun. Head left and circle 12,531-foot St. Louis Lake before heading back the way you came.

Trail Mix

This low-cost, high-energy snack is easy to make and perfect for munching on while hiking. Just pick any combination of the following ingredients, throw everything in a bag, shake it all up, and your good to go. Mix, match, get creative!

- Granola
- Nuts, such as sunflower seeds, peanuts, cashews, brazil nuts, or almonds
- Chocolate, white chocolate, or butterscotch chips
- Dried fruit, such as apricots, raisins, cranberries, apples, mangos, papaya, pineapple, or bananas
- Have fun! Add dried coconut, candied ginger, chocolate-covered toffee pieces, malt balls, or your favorite bite-sized treat!

Apex Park

Apex/Pick 'n Sledge/Sluicebox

Distance 4.5-mile balloon loop

Difficulty Moderate

Elevation Gain 1,000 feet

Dogs On leash

Directions From Denver, head west on I-70. Head west again on US 40. Turn left onto Heritage Rd. and continue to trailhead, which is adjacent to Heritage Square. Park by northeast corner of paved area.

Highlights Panoramic views; creek; wildflowers

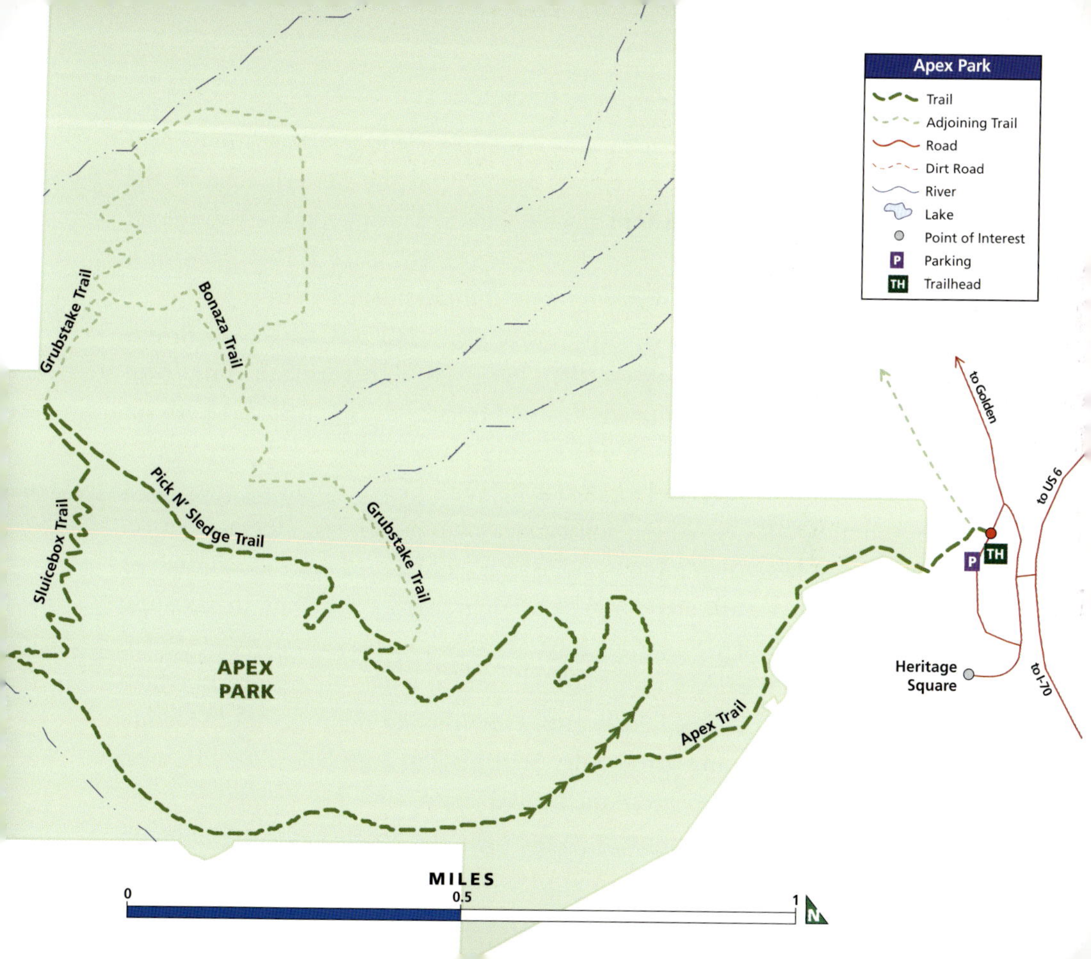
Apex Park
Trail
Adjoining Trail
Road
Dirt Road
River
Lake
Point of Interest
Parking
Trailhead
Grubstake Trail
Bonaza Trail
Pick N' Sledge Trail
Grubstake Trail
Sluicebox Trail
APEX PARK
Apex Trail
to Golden
to US 6
to I-70
Heritage Square
P
TH
MILES
0
0.5
1
N

With a humble beginning adjacent to the Heritage Square Amusement Park/Shopping Center just off I-70 on the western edge of the Denver metroplex, **Apex Trail** quickly leads to a ravine threaded by a small creek. Parking for this Jefferson County Open Space Park is generous. Arrive early to beat summer-afternoon thunderstorm activity.

Pick up an Apex Gulch brochure at the metal box on the northwest edge of the lower parking lot, then head west under orphan elms. Turn right, crossing an intentionally rusted bridge. Take the first dirt path on the left, which bears a small sign reading "Apex Trail."

The 4.5-mile balloon loop heads up Apex Gulch following the sound of running water. Avoid the polished leaves of poison ivy—leaves of three, leave them be. When a big wooden sign emblazoned with a trail map of 770-acre Apex Park arrives on your right, take a moment to note the Apex/Pick 'n Sledge/Sluicebox loop.

Apex Trail rises over rocky ground until it comes to a junction where the loop portion of the hike begins. Head up and right on **Pick 'n Sledge Trail.** The track climbs across a dry, south-facing slope before leveling a bit to reach a panoramic view of the Denver-metro area. The distant cityscape is flanked by Green Mountain on the right and South Table Mountain on the left.

Switchbacking westward, the trail continues its ascent, becoming rockier. Where the trail turns a corner to view the city and the plains beyond, note a long, white shape on the horizon looking like a solitary range of permanently snowcapped peaks: the Denver International Airport.

As the sounds of civilization disappear, the trail eases, passing a few lonely ponderosa pines. Soon, a junction sends **Grubstake Trail** right while this loop continues left on Pick 'n Sledge Trail. The rocky, rising trail finally levels where it briefly enters the shade of Douglas firs.

At the next junction, angle left onto **Sluicebox Trail.** Grubstake Trail is to the right. A number of switchbacks take the track down to intersect Apex Trail. Head left, following the intermittent creek downstream.

Fun Fact

Apex Gulch used to be a strategic stop for miners and suppliers. The frontier settlement included a toll road that was one of the earliest routes to the mines of Central City, previously known as the Gregory Diggings. Here the miners could rest for the long journey and get supplies before heading up into the mountains.

Under narrow-leaved cottonwoods, Apex Trail touches the creek, passing to the right of a large outcrop. Travel through extensive thickets of wild plum, hawthorn, and chokecherry, staying right to retrace the loop's "string" back to the parking area.

Lower Chicago Lake

Distance	10.0 miles roundtrip
Difficulty	Moderate to strenuous
Elevation Gain	1,060 feet
Dogs	On leash
Directions	From Denver, take I-70 west to exit 240. Go south on CO 103 for to reach the Echo Lake access road. Trailhead parking is located where the road dead-ends.
Highlights	Mountain lake; creek; high-mountain views; wildflowers

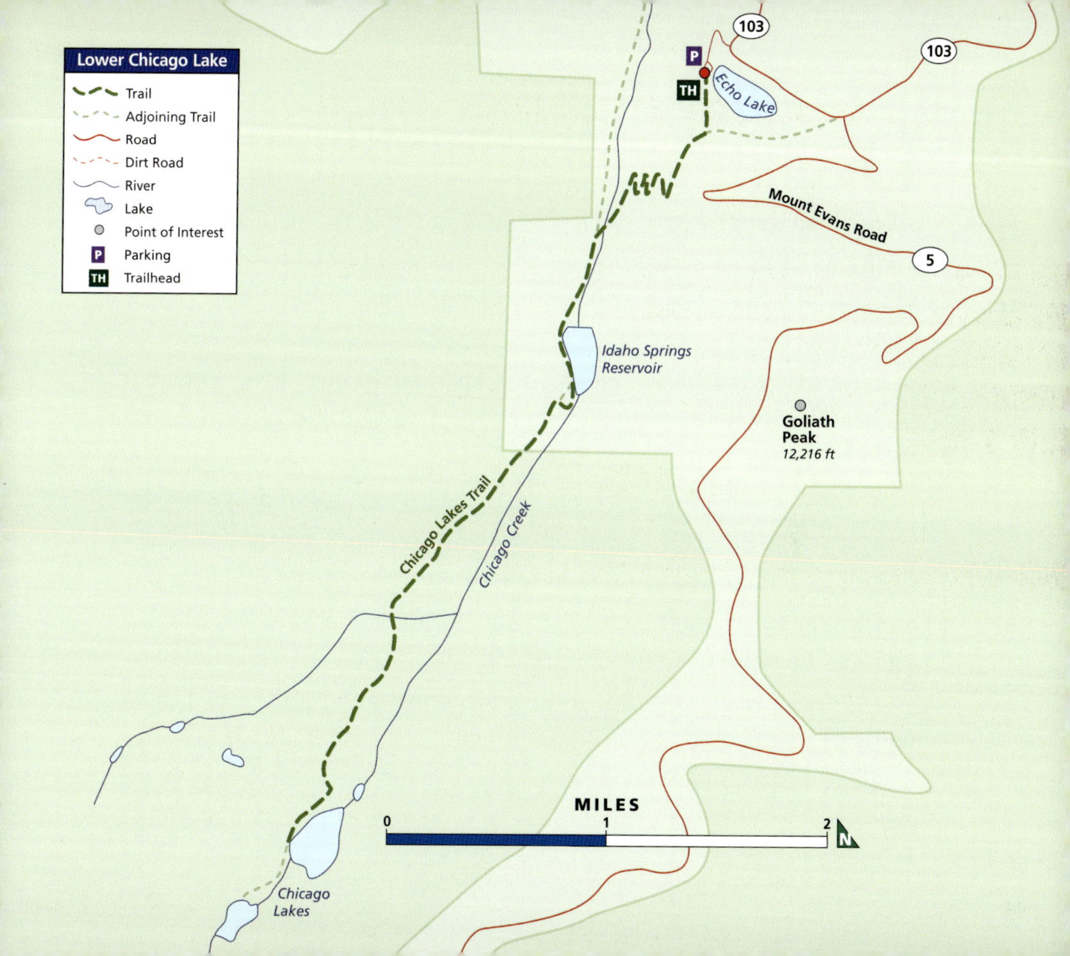

Lower Chicago Lake
Trail
Adjoining Trail
Road
Dirt Road
River
Lake
Point of Interest
Parking
Trailhead
103
103
P
TH
Echo Lake
Mount Evans Road
5
Idaho Springs Reservoir
Goliath Peak
12,216 ft
Chicago Lakes Trail
Chicago Creek
Chicago Lakes
MILES
0
1
2
N

Discovering Lower Chicago Lake is like finding a 10-acre emerald. Set within a circlet of pewter peaks, it is your reward for having hiked 5 miles. You'll descend over 400 feet before beginning the main ascent, thus having to regain that elevation by hike's end. Altogether, this scenic hike is one of the best. Boots are highly recommended; hiking poles can be handy too.

Early arrival is advised, not only for a parking place at Echo Lake, but to avoid those wild summer-afternoon thunderstorms that can arrive with lightning speed.

At the east side of the parking area, a cabled gate sports a sign for this Denver Mountain Park. Head up to the picnic area, where Echo Lake spreads out before you. Turn right to locate a small sign pointing the way to **Chicago Lakes Trail,** then follow the lakeshore briefly before another sign, on the right, ushers you into the forest.

The trail rises briefly, then drifts down only to rise again over a rocky footbed. Snatch glimpses of distant mountains between the surrounding conifers. Bristlecone pines cling to ledgy granite on a steep, west-facing exposure. Opening to the south is the colorful maw of 14,265-foot Mount Evans.

Pass under rugged outcrops and jumbled rock to reach a small national forest boundary sign. Make your way down to a series of long, rocky switchbacks that carry you to Chicago Creek, where sturdy half-logs facilitate a crossing. The trail leads to a road; turn left and follow it a mile up to the Idaho Springs Reservoir. Continue along the west side of the lake. At the far end Chicago Lakes Trail returns to single track where a sign announces that you are in Mount Evans Wilderness. Climb immediately into an area burned long ago by wildfire.

Continue along, hiking in and out of the burned area. Hidden Chicago Creek sounds off, and nearby, great cliffs of sheer granite are topped with treeless tundra. Cruise past standing and downed snags softened by wildflowers and healthy grasses. Cross a waterway on convenient stones.

Mini First-Aid Kit

- Bandages
- Ibuprofen or other pain relievers/anti-inflammatories
- Anti-bacterial towelettes
- Burn ointment
- Blister kit or moleskin

A plastic soapbox makes a good container for these.

The trail eases through a forested area and, at last, emerges into a realm of towering mountains. Behold Lower Chicago Lake shimmering in its verdant bowl under the rugged brows of lofty summits. Dip your feet in the lake's cool waters, and enjoy a snack while watching for trout.

Mount Goliath Natural Area

Walter Pesman Trail

Distance 3.0 miles roundtrip, including keyhole loop

Difficulty Moderate to strenuous

Elevation Gain 612 feet

Dogs On leash

Directions From Denver, take I-70 west to exit 240. Head south on CO 103/Mount Evans Highway for 14 miles to Echo Lake. Turn right on CO 5/Mt. Evans Road and go 2.9 miles to the parking lot on the left at the lower trailhead.

Fees & Info $10 day pass

Highlights Ancient bristlecone pines; spectacular rock gardens; alpine tundra; opportunity to summit nearby fourteener Mount Evans

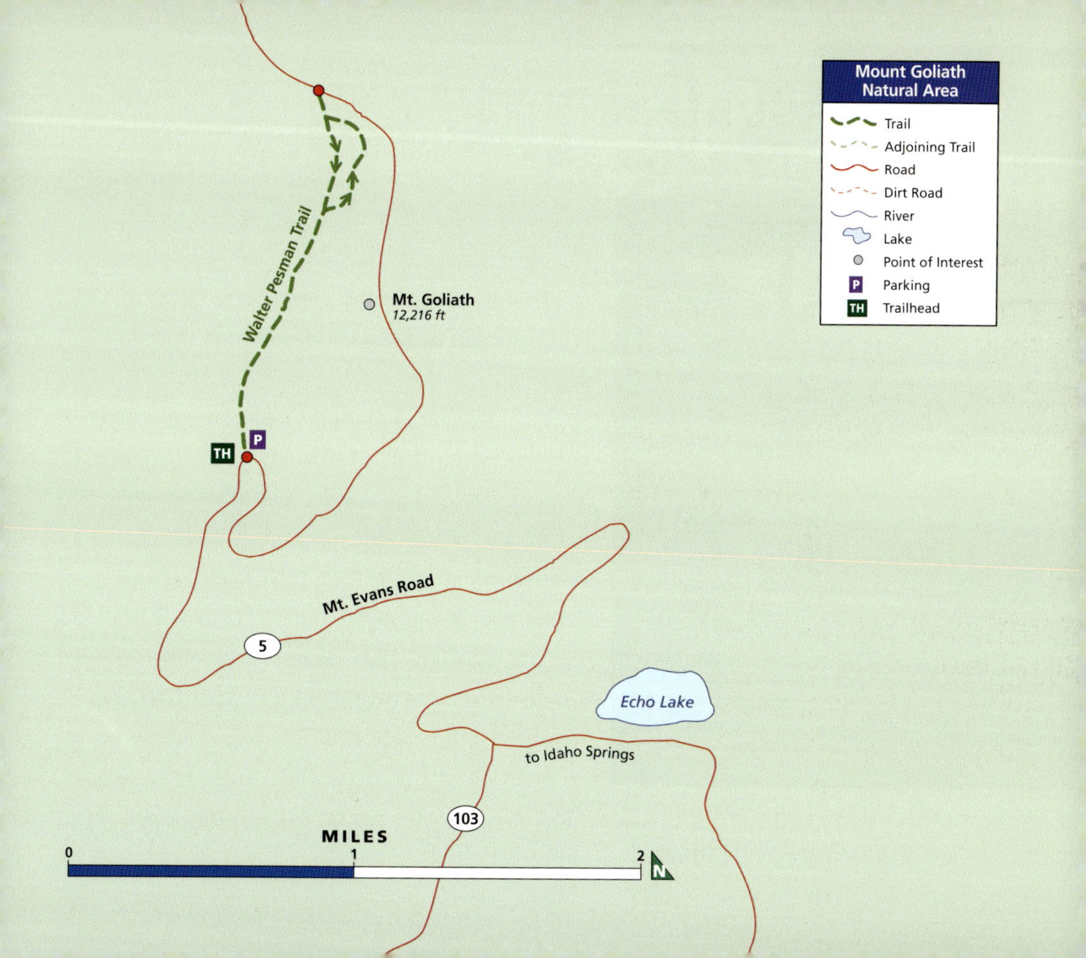

Mount Goliath Natural Area
Trail
Adjoining Trail
Road
Dirt Road
River
Lake
Point of Interest
Parking
Trailhead
Walter Pesman Trail
Mt. Goliath
12,216 ft
TH
P
Mt. Evans Road
5
Echo Lake
to Idaho Springs
103
MILES
0
1
2
N

An amazing hiking opportunity awaits on this sub-peak of fourteener Mount Evans. Though the distance is not great, the elevation puts the hike in the moderate to strenuous category. There is 33 percent less available oxygen at this altitude than at sea level.

The **Walter Pesman Trail** begins in conifers, then quickly thrusts you into an ancient world. This world is contorted, colorful, and admirable—you'll pass bristlecone pines that are well into their second millennia. Bristlecone pine can reach an age greater than that of any other known single living organism. The oldest, a tree named Methuselah, is 4,789 years old.

Switchbacks lead to widening views as the trail becomes more steep. You'll eventually reach the tundra, where trees are absent and flowers and grasses are dominant.

Pocket rock gardens prepare the way for one of Colorado's finest gardens, the Alpine Garden Loop. Turn right when you reach the junction and head counterclockwise around the loop. You'll pass among giant boulders and attendant wildflowers. A stellar view opens up, featuring Mt. Evans, Mt. Bierstadt, and Grays and Torreys Peaks, all fourteeners. The latter two straddle the Continental Divide. Complete the loop, then retrace your steps back to your car.

When you're finished with your hike, why not bag a fourteener? Hop back in your car and continue up the Mount Evans Highway—North America's highest paved road—to where it ends at the summit parking area. Then hike a few hundred feet to stand on Mount Evans' rocky 14,280-foot summit.

Fun Fact

You'll find bristlecone pines in Mount Goliath Natural Area that are more than 1,500 years old! Many of them range from between 900 to 1,500 years old, making this bristlecone forest one of the oldest forests around. You can learn more about these trees by stopping in at the Dos Chappell Nature Center during your visit to the area.

Butler Gulch

Distance 5.0 miles roundtrip

Difficulty Moderate to strenuous

Elevation Gain 1,240 feet

Dogs On leash

Directions From Denver, take I-70 west to US 40 W. Continue on US 40 to Henderson Mine Rd. Head left and continue 2.5 miles to Jones Pass Rd. Go right and continue 0.5 miles. Parking is on the left at the trailhead.

Highlights Over 100 wildflower species from July to early September; Continental Divide; colorful Vasquez Peak

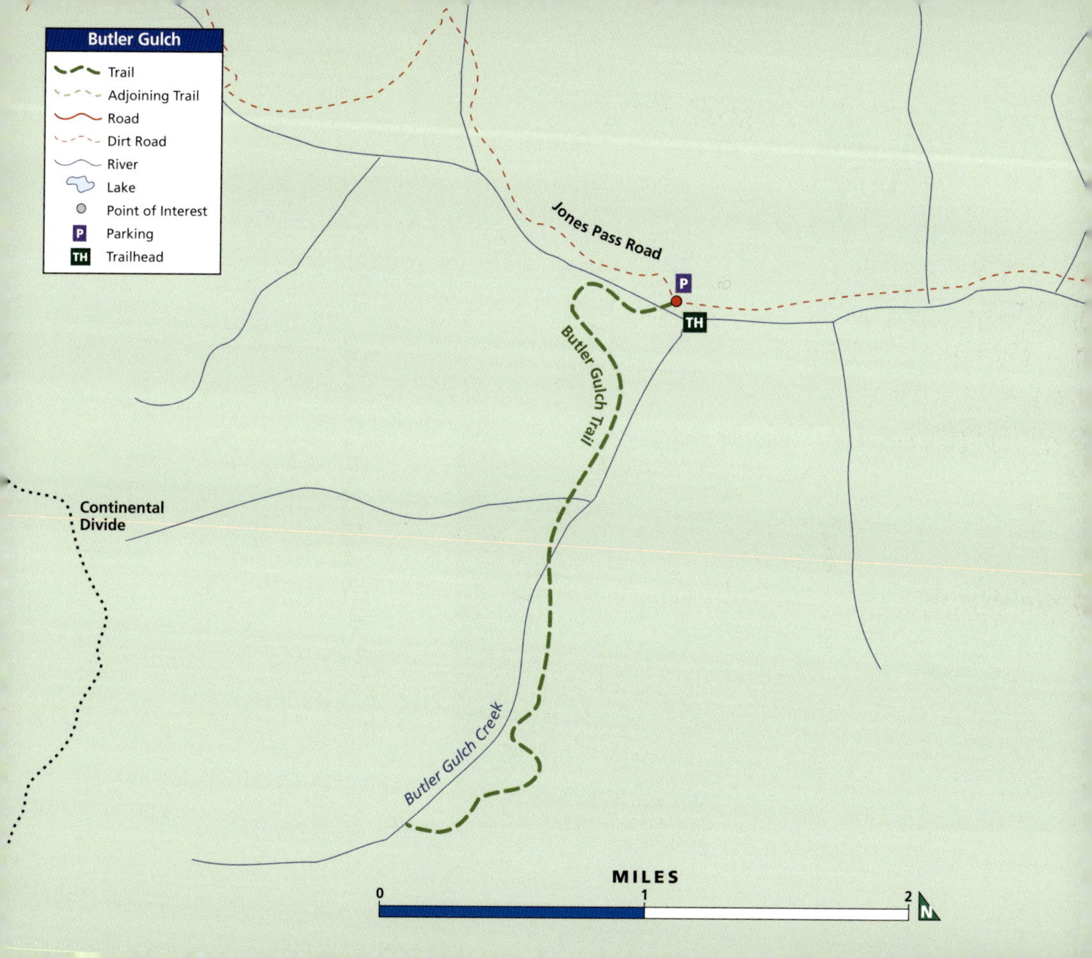
Butler Gulch
Trail
Adjoining Trail
Road
Dirt Road
River
Lake
Point of Interest
Parking
Trailhead
Jones Pass Road
P
TH
Butler Gulch Trail
Continental Divide
Butler Gulch Creek
MILES
0
1
2
N

A prime hike, the 2.5-mile **Butler Gulch Trail** is not only floriferous, but also scenic, adventuresome, and aerobic. This beautiful trek, located west of Berthoud Pass Road off Jones Pass Road, climbs to a wide-open bowl cradled by the Continental Divide. Altitude and elevation gain give Butler Gulch its moderate to strenuous rating.

Parking is extremely limited, so arrive early. The goal cirque is above tree-line and exposed to those wild summer-afternoon thunderstorms. A rain jacket might come in handy.

Walk around the big gate where Butler Gulch Trail starts and take the old roadway across a rushing creek. The eroded, rising track becomes rocky and continues to a challenging stream crossing. This is not the first, nor the last crossing you will face.

One of the many switchbacks reveals a gap in the coniferous forest that frames colorful 12,947-foot Vasquez Peak to the north. Continue on, until suddenly you find yourself out in the open—in late July, brilliant waves of flowers welcome you to Butler Gulch. Rugged, snow-crested, sweeping peaks push 13,000 feet, creating a magnificent mountainscape.

An easing slope along an overgrown roadway allows you to view talus that nurtures Colorado blue columbine. These rocky slopes are home to the high-pitched pika. Perky and round-eared, this member of the ancient order of rabbits and hares is always busy.

Hike Smart

When you're hiking in Colorado's high country, getting lost or separated from your group can be extremely dangerous. Be sure to plan ahead for such emergencies and take a whistle, two-way walkie-talkie, or cell phone (make sure you'll have service) with you. If you plan on hiking alone, always tell someone you trust where you're going and when you plan to be back by.

As you climb higher, you are reacquainted with tumbling Butler Gulch Creek encompassed by Continental Divide peaks. Turn around here, or, if you want more miles, cross the creek and continue climbing up to the cirque. You'll pass tumbledown mining cabins along the way.

Herman Gulch

Distance	6.8 miles roundtrip
Difficulty	Moderate to strenuous
Elevation Gain	1,500 feet
Dogs	On leash
Directions	From Denver, go west on I-70 to exit 218. The parking area is on your right.
Highlights	Mountain lake; diverse and plentiful wildflowers; grand high-country scenery

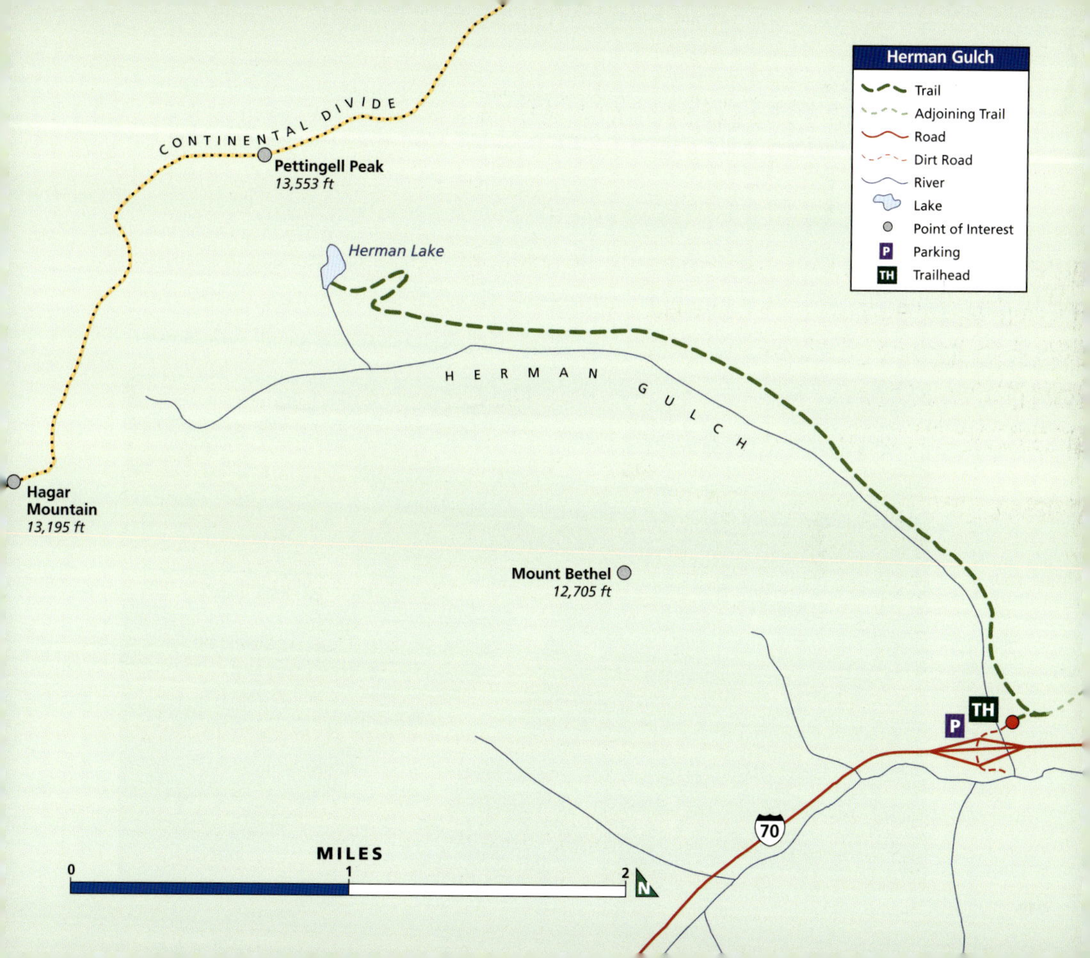

Herman Gulch
Trail
Adjoining Trail
Road
Dirt Road
River
Lake
Point of Interest
P Parking
TH Trailhead
CONTINENTAL DIVIDE
Pettingell Peak
13,553 ft
Herman Lake
Hagar Mountain
13,195 ft
HERMAN GULCH
Mount Bethel
12,705 ft
TH
P
70
MILES
0
1
2
N

So beloved is convenient **Herman Gulch Trail** that the parking lot has been enlarged more than once; restrooms were added recently as well. Hike on a weekday to avoid crowds.

Part of the hike's charm is the grand, though unfortunately shrinking, displays of Colorado blue columbine in mid- to late June. This trail's grand scenery, aerobic challenge, and 100 species of resident wildflowers

add equally to the charm, as does odd-colored Herman Lake, where the route ends.

The route begins gently on a path of crusher fines. You'll soon reach a fork where the Herman Gulch Trail bears left and the **Watrous Gulch Trail** goes right. Stay left. The pitch steepens before easing again, entering deep shade. Pass springs and streamlets nurturing fringed grass of Parnassus and fragrant white bog orchids.

> **Local Scene**
>
> The hike will make you hungry, so stop in historic Idaho Springs and try the Buffalo Restaurant & Bar (buffalorestaurant.com) or Beau Jo's Pizza (beaujos.com). The Tommyknocker Brewery (tommyknocker.com) serves up award-winning microbrew beer and classic pub fare.

A broad columbine-charged meadow opens to a view of 13,553-foot Pettingell Peak. Cross a split-log bridge, then head up through pocket meadows. Top a rougher pitch to reach a level space where stunted Engelmann spruce form patches. Pass a small pond on the right. Check nearby lingering snowbanks for impatient snow buttercup, which may bloom faster than the snow melts.

Push on to celadon-green Herman Lake with its waterfall inlet and thick alpine meadows. All around you, thirteeners cut the skyline. Find a handy boulder to perch on, and enjoy this Rocky Mountain high.

Mount Bierstadt

Distance 6.0 miles roundtrip

Difficulty Strenuous

Elevation Gain 2,930 feet

Dogs On leash

Directions From Boulder, take Broadway St./CO 93 south. Make a slight left onto US 6 and go 2.8 miles. Merge onto CO 470 E toward Colorado Springs and go 0.7 mile. Exit onto I-70 W toward Grand Junction and continue for 32 miles. Take exit 228 to Georgetown. Follow the signs to Guanella Pass and drive 12 miles to a spacious trailhead parking area at the top of the pass.

Highlights Good first-time fourteener; panoramic views; easily accessible

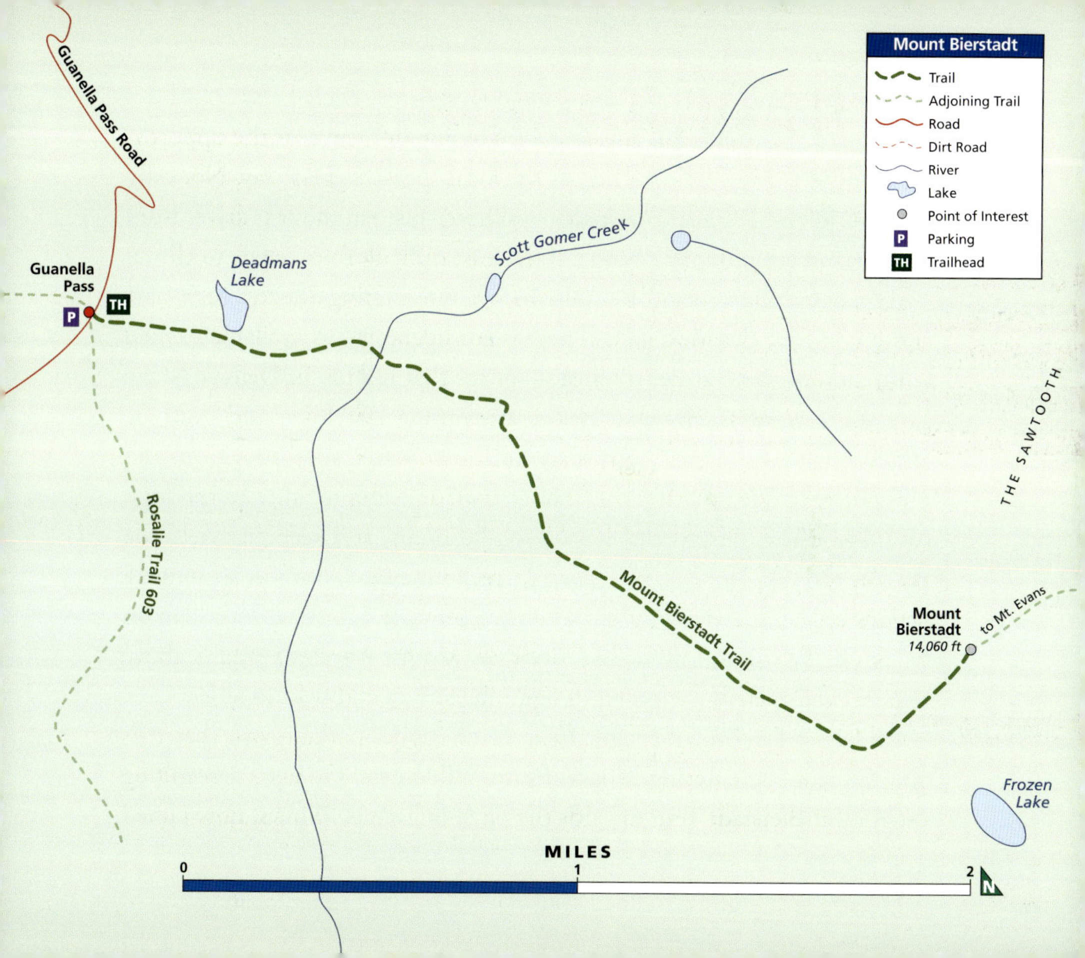
Mount Bierstadt
Trail
Adjoining Trail
Road
Dirt Road
River
Lake
Point of Interest
Parking
Trailhead
Guanella Pass Road
Guanella Pass
P
TH
Deadmans Lake
Scott Gomer Creek
THE SAWTOOTH
Rosalie Trail 603
Mount Bierstadt Trail
Mount Bierstadt
14,060 ft
to Mt. Evans
Frozen Lake
MILES
0
1
2
N

One of the wonderful advantages of basing in Denver is the opportunity to "bag" a fourteener, as the local "peak baggers" say. Not only is 14,065-foot Mount Bierstadt's trailhead just an hour's drive from Denver, but the mountain is one of the least difficult fourteeners to climb.

This description assigns the ascent a strenuous rating due to a high start and 2,930-foot elevation gain. There is considerably less available oxygen at the summit than at the trailhead—or for that matter, in Denver. Make sure you are well acclimated before attempting this hike, and don't be afraid to take rest stops. Don't forget adequate water, sun protection, and outdoor gear. The weather can change with amazing rapidity in the high country—check the forecast before you head out, and keep an eye to the sky. An early morning start is strongly recommended, not just to secure a parking spot, but also to beat out summer afternoon thunderstorms. Plan on being off the summit by noon. All of the **Mount Bierstadt Trail** is above treeline, and therefore exposed to lightning strikes and wild weather.

To begin, head for the signed gap in the upper parking area that tells you that you are entering Mount Evans Wilderness. Go east, descending the Mount Bierstadt Trail towards the once-infamous willows, now tamed by a series of volunteer-built boardwalks. Carving the skyline is the Sawtooth, a ridge that connects Mount Bierstadt to another fourteener, Mount Evans. Soon, you will cross Scott Gomer Creek. Willow-girt zigzags lift the trail past the last Engelmann spruces. Fabulous views greet the eye.

Listen for the distinctive call of pika, a member of the rabbit and hare family that favors rocky boulder fields. Mountain goats also make their home at these heights, and tundra plants cushion the slopes. The trail wends steadily up Bierstadt's northwest shoulder. From here, the pitch gets serious and the tread rockier.

Arrive at a saddle, the far side of which reveals Frozen Lake far below. Choose rocks carefully as you scramble up them on the last pitch. Once atop, reward yourself with a stunning 360-degree panorama that includes Grays and Torreys Peaks—Colorado's only fourteeners straddling the Continental Divide.

Hike Smart

Make sure not to push yourself too hard in the beginning, as you not only have to hike in, but you also have to hike back out. Take frequent short breaks. Long breaks allow the muscles to stiffen. A shorter stride will help keep your oxygen intake more even, which is ever more crucial as you tackle the summit, where there is 40 percent less oxygen than at sea level.

Mount Sniktau

Distance	3.5 miles roundtrip
Difficulty	Strenuous
Elevation Gain	1,235 feet
Dogs	On leash
Directions	From Denver, take I-70 west to exit 216/ Loveland Pass/US 6. Go south 4 miles on US 6. Park on the left (east) side of the pass.
Highlights	Blooming tundra; good introductory thirteener; 360-degree views

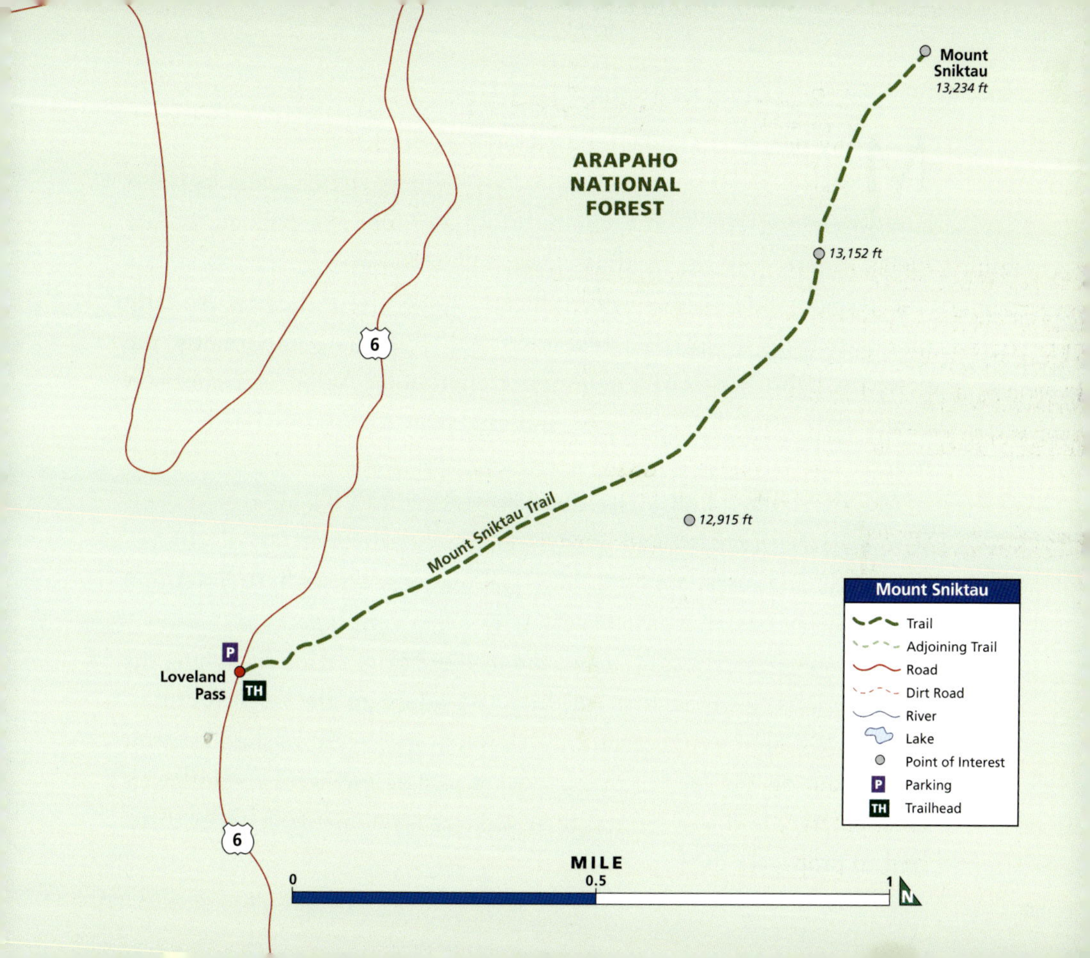
Mount
Sniktau
13,234 ft
ARAPAHO
NATIONAL
FOREST
13,152 ft
6
Mount Sniktau Trail
12,915 ft
P
Loveland
Pass
TH
6
Mount Sniktau
Trail
Adjoining Trail
Road
Dirt Road
River
Lake
Point of Interest
Parking
Trailhead
MILE
0
0.5
1
N

Many people enjoy the regal panorama afforded them on the top of nearly 12,000-foot Loveland Pass. Others stretch their legs and lungs by hiking east, to the summit of 13,235-foot Mt. Sniktau. In late June and early July, the tundra is in gem-like bloom.

Parking on fine weather weekends gets competitive at the pass. An early hike start helps avoid the competition and, even more importantly, the powerful lightning storms of summer afternoons. Wind is a common companion at this lofty elevation and can create a substantial chill factor, so layer up.

Mount Sniktau Trail leaves the east parking area where a prominent sign declares that Loveland Pass is on the Continental Divide. Immediately the trail forks, but both tines rejoin shortly. The right or lower trail is a less strenuous, more sheltered way to begin your hike.

The trails converge shortly and the incline begins seriously. Taking the steep sections slowly at first will help you adjust to the rarefied atmosphere. Early summer is a good time to watch insects flit to the tiny gems that bloom on the harsh tundra. Within a mere 6-8 weeks, wildflowers must emerge, bud and bloom, then wait for a pollinator in order to set seed to propagate their species.

The rocky knolls along the way are great places to catch your breath. Take in the fabulous peripheral views that practically beg for you to turn all the way around, so as not to miss any of the memorable mountainscape. Don't forget to look down. At your feet, tundra cushions, buns, and mats display enchanting seasonal flowers.

By the third well-carined knoll, the sky seems higher and wider, the vistas awesome and stretching nearly forever. Range after range skewer the skyline, supporting the fact that Colorado is the highest state overall.

Continue on along the broad ridgeline. Be aware that high winds can make this route dangerous—turn around if necessary. The fifth knoll marks the summit. Look for a summit register in the wind shelter and add your name. Thirteeners rise into the skyline around you, and off to the southeast you can spot two famous fourteeners, Grays and Torreys.

Ten Hiking Essentials

- Map
- Compass
- Flashlight
- Extra food
- Water and water purification apparatus (a bottle filter or chemical tablets are good options)
- Rain Gear and extra clothing (avoid cotton because it keeps moisture close to the skin—a plastic poncho is your best bet)
- Matches and a fire starter (a candle works nicely)
- Sun protection and sunglasses (this is extremely important in Colorado)
- Pocket knife or multi-purpose tool
- First aid kit

For additional hiking ideas, check out the following publications:

Erickson, Bette. *Best Boulder Region Hiking Trails.* Englewood, Colo.: Westcliffe Publishers, 2005.

Erickson, Bette. *Forever Young, a Hiking Guide.* Broomfield, Colo.: CG Press, 2003.

Fielder, John. *John Fielder's Best of Colorado,* 2nd ed. Englewood, Colo.: Westcliffe Publishers, 2007.

Irwin, Pamela and David Harlan. *100 Best Denver Area and Front Range Day Hikes.* Englewood, Colo.: Westcliffe Publishers, 2007.

About the Author

Pam Irwin, pictured with her husband, photographer David Irwin, is an avid hiker and has been a volunteer naturalist at Roxborough State Park since the early 1980s. Her extensive background in and love of wildflower identification has earned her the certified title of Native Plant Master from Colorado State University. Pamela is also a member of the Rocky Mountain Nature Association, the Rocky Mountain Chapter of the American Rock Garden Society, Windflowers Garden Club, and the Audubon Society.

La gallinita roja

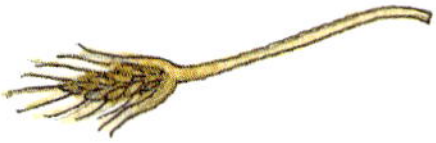

Una gallinita roja estaba picoteando en el patio cuando se encontró un grano de trigo.

–¡Miren lo que me he encontrado! -exclamó.

Vinieron el pato, la vaca y el gato y todos miraron el grano de trigo.

–¿Quién quiere venir conmigo a sembrar el grano de trigo? -preguntó la gallinita roja.

–Yo, no -dijo el pato.

–Yo, no -dijo la vaca.

–Yo, no -dijo el gato.

–Pues si nadie quiere ayudarme, yo sola lo sembraré -dijo la gallinita roja y se fue sola a sembrar su grano de trigo.

Cuando el trigo estuvo crecido y maduro, la gallinita roja preguntó:

–¿Quién quiere ir conmigo a cosechar el trigo?

–Yo, no -dijo el pato.

–Yo, no -dijo la vaca.

–Yo, no -dijo el gato.

–Pues si nadie quiere ayudarme, yo sola lo cosecharé -dijo la gallinita roja y se fue sola a cosechar el trigo.

Cuando el trigo estuvo cosechado, la gallinita roja preguntó:

–¿Quién quiere ir conmigo al molino a moler trigo?

–Yo, no -dijo el pato.

–Yo, no -dijo la vaca.

–Yo, no -dijo el gato.

–Pues si nadie quiere ayudarme, yo sola iré al molino -dijo la gallinita roja y se fue sola a moler el trigo.

Cuando el trigo estuvo molido y hecho harina, la gallinita roja preguntó:

–¿Quién quiere venir conmigo a amasar la harina para hacer pan?

–Yo, no -dijo el pato.

–Yo, no -dijo la vaca.

–Yo, no -dijo el gato.

–Pues si nadie quiere ayudarme, yo sola amasaré la harina -dijo la gallinita roja y se fue sola a hacer el pan.

Cuando el pan estuvo cocido, dorado y oloroso, la gallinita roja preguntó:

–¿Quién quiere venir conmigo a comer el pan?

–¡Yo quiero! -graznó el pato.

–¡Yo quiero! -mugió la vaca.

–¡Yo quiero! -maulló el gato.

–¡Pues no! -dijo la gallinita roja-. El pan yo sola me lo comeré.

Ricitos de Oro y los tres osos

Había una vez tres osos que vivían en una casita en medio del bosque. Papá Oso era un oso grande, grandote. Mamá Osa era una osa mediana. Y Osito era un oso pequeñito.

Un día, Mamá Osa preparó avena con miel para el desayuno y la vació en tres pocillos. Mientras se enfriaba, salieron los tres osos a dar un paseo por el bosque.

Miel

Entonces, una niña llamada Ricitos de Oro llegó hasta la casa de los osos. Se acercó, y como la puerta estaba entreabierta, se asomó y espió por la rendija. Miró hacia un lado y hacia el otro, y como no vio a nadie, decidió entrar.

Al ver la mesa puesta con los tres pocillos de avena, sintió mucha hambre.

Probó la avena del pocillo grande, grandote y estaba demasiado caliente.

Probó la avena del pocillo mediano y estaba demasiado espesa.

Probó la avena del pocillo pequeñito y estaba tan rica, que se la comió toda.

Luego, Ricitos de Oro quiso sentarse a descansar.

Se sentó en la silla grande, grandota, pero era muy alta.

Se sentó en la silla mediana, pero era muy ancha.

Se sentó en la silla pequeñita y la encontró a su gusto. Pero la silla era demasiado pequeña y se rompió.

Entonces, Ricitos de Oro sintió sueño y quiso acostarse a dormir. Subió las escaleras y vio tres camas.

Se acostó en la cama grande, grandota y la encontró muy dura.

Se acostó en la cama mediana y la

encontró muy blanda.

Se acostó en la cama pequeñita y la encontró tan sabrosa, que se quedó dormida inmediatamente.

Los tres osos regresaron de su paseo.

Papá Oso vio una cuchara en su pocillo y rugió con voz de trueno:

–¡Alguien ha probado mi avena!

Mamá Osa vio una cuchara en su pocillo y gruñó con voz de granizo:

–¡Alguien ha probado mi avena!

Osito miró su pocillo y lloró:

–¡Alguien se ha comido toda mi avena!

Papá Oso fue hasta su silla, vio que el

cojín estaba torcido y rugió con voz de trueno:

–¡Alguien se ha sentado en mi silla!

Mamá Osa fue hasta su silla, vio que el cojín estaba torcido y gruñó con voz de granizo:

–¡Alguien se ha sentado en mi silla!

Osito miró su silla y lloró:

–¡Alguien ha roto mi silla!

Entonces, los tres osos subieron las escaleras.

Papá Oso vio su cama revuelta y rugió con voz de trueno:

–¡Alguien se ha acostado en mi cama!

Mamá Osa vio su cama revuelta y gruñó con voz de granizo:

–¡Alguien se ha acostado en mi cama!

Osito miró su cama y lloró:

–¡Alguien está durmiendo en mi cama!

Ricitos de Oro se despertó asustada al oír los gritos. Saltó de la cama, bajó volando las escaleras y corrió y corrió hasta que salió del bosque.

Y más nunca regresó a la casa de los tres osos.

Los siete chivitos

Había una vez siete chivitos blancos que vivían con su mamá en una casa en el bosque. Pero en el bosque vivía también el lobo malvado.

Un día, la mamá tuvo que ir al mercado. Llamó a sus siete chivitos y les dijo:

–Cierren bien la puerta y no le abran a nadie, porque el lobo malvado puede venir.

–¿Y cómo sabremos que es el lobo malvado el que toca a la puerta? -preguntaron los chivitos.

–Porque el lobo tiene la voz ronca y las patas negras -contestó la mamá y se despidió.

Al quedarse solos, los siete chivitos cerraron la puerta con candado.

El lobo, que estaba escondido detrás de unas matas, vio pasar a la chiva camino del pueblo y pensó: "Ahora me comeré a los siete chivitos que están tiernos y gorditos".

En tres saltos llegó a la puerta de la casa y tocó: *¡Tun, tun, tun!*

–¿Quién es?

–Abran, mis chivitos. Soy su mamá y les traigo caramelos del mercado -dijo el lobo.

Pero los chivitos le contestaron:

–No, tú no eres nuestra mamá. Ella tiene la voz clarita y tú la tienes ronca.

Entonces, el lobo se fue a su casa y se tomó seis cucharadas de miel para aclararse la voz. Regresó a casa de los chivitos. *¡Tun, tun, tun!*

–¿Quién es?

–Abran, mis chivitos. Soy su mamá y les traigo caramelos del mercado -dijo el lobo con una voz clarita.

Los chivitos iban a abrirle la puerta, cuando vieron las patas por la rendija.

–No, tú no eres nuestra mamá. Ella tiene las patas blancas y tú las tienes negras.

El lobo se puso furioso. Entonces, se fue a casa del molinero y le pidió que le echara harina en las patas hasta que estuvieron blancas. El molinero le echó harina y más harina en las patas hasta que estuvieron blancas. El lobo regresó corriendo a casa de los chivitos. *¡Tun, tun, tun!*

–¿Quién es?

–Abran, mis chivitos. Soy su mamá y

les traigo caramelos del mercado -dijo el lobo.

–Queremos ver tus patas primero -contestaron los chivitos.

Y el lobo asomó sus patas enharinadas por la rendija. Los chivitos, entonces, abrieron la puerta. El lobo brincó dentro de la casa. Todos corrieron a esconderse.

El primer chivito se metió en la cesta de ropa; el segundo chivito, debajo de la cama; el tercer chivito, en una gaveta; el cuarto chivito, debajo de la mesa; el quinto chivito, en el aparador; el sexto chivito, detrás del sofá, y el más chiquito se metió en la caja del reloj.

Pero el lobo malvado los fue encontrando uno por uno, y uno por uno se los fue comiendo. Menos al más chiquito porque no se le ocurrió mirar dentro del reloj.

El lobo se fue con la barrigota llena y se acostó a dormir la siesta debajo de un árbol en medio del bosque.

Cuando la chiva regresó del mercado, encontró la puerta abierta y la casa toda revuelta.

–Ay, mis hijos. ¡Ay, mis chivitos! ¡El lobo malvado me los ha comido a todos!

–¡A mí no! ¡A mí no! -gritó el más chiquito desde el reloj.

La chiva lo ayudó a salir y el chivito le contó lo que había pasado. La chiva, entonces, buscó tijeras, el carrete de hilo, la aguja y el dedal, tomó a su único chivito de la mano y se fue al bosque a buscar al lobo.

Caminaron y caminaron hasta que escucharon unos ronquidos. Y ahí, durmiendo debajo de un árbol, vieron al lobo.

La chiva se acercó calladita, y de un tijeretazo le abrió la barriga. Afuera saltaron los chivitos, uno por uno. El

lobo estaba durmiendo tan profundamente, que no se daba cuenta de nada. Los chivitos brincaban felices, pero la chiva les dijo:

–*Shhhhh...* no vayan a despertar al lobo que aún no hemos terminado. Busquen seis piedras bien grandes para llenarle la barriga.

Así lo hicieron y luego la chiva enhebró la aguja y, con mucho cuidado, cosió la barriga.

La chiva y sus chivitos regresaron a la casa, trancaron la puerta y se comieron los caramelos que la mamá había traído del mercado.

Y el lobo, mientras tanto, despertó con dolor de barriga. Quiso ir a tomar agua al río y se paró todo patuleco. La barriga le pesaba muchísimo.

–*¡Ayyy!* Estos chivitos no estaban tan tiernos -se quejó el lobo.

Y cuando se inclinó a la orilla del río a beber, con el peso de las piedras... *¡plaf!* el lobo cayó al agua.

La corriente se lo llevó, y la chiva y los chivitos no lo volvieron a ver jamás.

Los tres cochinitos

Había una vez tres cochinitos que decidieron salir a probar fortuna.

El primer cochinito se encontró por el camino con un granjero que cargaba un fardo de paja.

–Señor granjero -le dijo el cochinito-, ¿podrías regalarme un poco de paja para construir mi casa?

–Con mucho gusto -dijo el granjero y

le regaló un poco de paja.

El cochinito comenzó a construir su casa, *pijjj pajjj, pijjj pajjj,* y mientras trabajaba, cantaba:

En mi casa de paja viviré

y si el lobo viene,

no le abriré.

En un día estuvo lista. El cochinito la miró y le pareció que había quedado muy bonita. Entró contento a su casa y cerró la puerta.

El segundo cochinito se encontró por el camino con un leñador que llevaba un atado de palos.

–Señor leñador -le dijo el cochinito-,

¿podrías regalarme unos palos para construir mi casa?

–Con mucho gusto -dijo el leñador y le regaló unos palos.

El cochinito comenzó a construir su casa, *toqui ti toc, toqui ti toc,* y mientras trabajaba, cantaba:

En mi casa de palos viviré
y si el lobo viene,
no le abriré.

Se tardó cuatro días en terminarla. Cuando estuvo lista, el cochinito la miró y le pareció que había quedado muy bonita. Entró contento a su casa y cerró la puerta.

El tercer cochinito se encontró por el camino con un albañil que llevaba una carretilla de ladrillos.

-Señor albañil -le dijo el cochinito-, ¿podrías regalarme unos ladrillos para construir mi casa?

-Con mucho gusto -dijo el albañil y le regaló unos ladrillos.

El cochinito comenzó a construir su casa, *suishh suashh, suishh suashh,* y mientras trabajaba, cantaba:

En mi casa de ladrillos viviré
y si el lobo viene,
no le abriré.

Tardó más de una semana en terminarla.

Cuando estuvo lista, el cochinito la miró y le pareció que había quedado muy bonita y muy firme. Entró a su casa contento y satisfecho y cerró la puerta.

Llegó entonces el lobo a la casa de paja del primer cochinito y le dijo:

–Cochinito, invítame a pasar.

–No, lobo, a mi casa no podrás entrar -respondió el cochinito.

–Pues, ¡ya verás! Soplaré, soplaré y soplaré y tu casa de paja destrozaré.

El lobo tomó aire. Sopló, sopló y sopló, y la casa de paja voló por los aires.

El lobo dio un brinco para atrapar al cochinito, pero el cochinito salió co-

rriendo a esconderse en la casa de su hermano.

Llegó el lobo a la casa de palos del segundo cochinito y le dijo:

–Cochinito, invítame a pasar.

–No, lobo, a mi casa no podrás entrar -respondió el segundo cochinito.

–Pues, ¡ya verás! Soplaré, soplaré y soplaré y tu casa de palos destrozaré.

El lobo tomó aire. Sopló, sopló y sopló, y la casa de palos voló por los aires.

El lobo dio un brinco para atrapar a los dos cochinitos, pero los cochinitos salieron corriendo a esconderse en la casa de su hermano.

Llegó el lobo a la casa de ladrillos del tercer cochinito y dijo otra vez:

–Cochinito, invítame a pasar.

–No, lobo, a mi casa no podrás entrar -respondió el cochinito.

–Pues, ¡ya verás! Soplaré, soplaré y soplaré y tu casa de ladrillos destrozaré.

El lobo tomó mucho aire. Sopló, sopló y sopló, y la casa de ladrillos... no se movió.

El lobo, entonces, tomó mucho, muchísimo aire y sopló, sopló y resopló. Sopló más y más, y la casa de ladrillos... no se movió.

El lobo se puso bravo. Sopló con todas sus fuerzas hasta que ya no le quedó aire en los pulmones, y la casa de ladrillos del tercer cochinito... no se movió.

Lleno de furia, el lobo se subió a un árbol y del árbol brincó al techo de la casa de ladrillos. Comenzó a deslizarse por la chimenea. Pero los cochinitos habían puesto al fuego una gran olla de agua y cuando el lobo terminó de bajar por la chimenea, cayó justo en medio del agua hirviendo. Se peló enterito y salió escapando.

Y los tres cochinitos no lo volvieron a ver jamás.

Mediopollito

Una vez, una gallina se echó en su nido a empollar. Al cabo de veintiún días, los pollitos comenzaron a salir del cascarón. Nacieron nueve hermosos pollitos. Pero el último en romper el cascarón era muy extraño. Sólo tenía un ojo, un ala y una patica.

La mamá, al verlo, lo llamó Mediopollito.

Mediopollito brincaba por todo el corral detrás de sus hermanos, *tip tap, tip tap,* con su única patica, y hacía siempre lo que le daba la gana. Cuando la mamá llamaba a los pollitos, *clo cló, clo cló,* para que vinieran al nido, Mediopollito se escapaba. Cuando la mamá les enseñaba a escarbar y a picotear el suelo, Mediopollito se acostaba a dormir.

Un día, Mediopollito le dijo a su mamá:

–Estoy fastidiado de este corral. Me voy al palacio a ver al rey.

–El palacio queda muy lejos -le dijo la mamá- y tú eres muy pequeñito para viajar solo. No vayas ahora. Algún día, yo te llevaré.

Pero Mediopollito no quería esperar, así que meneó su media cabecita y dijo:

–Me iré hoy mismo.

Y así fue. *Tip tap, tip tap*, se alejó del corral brincando con su única patica.

Pronto, Mediopollito se encontró con un arroyo que estaba lleno de malezas.

–Mediopollito -le dijo el arroyo-, ayúdame. Quita estas malezas con tu medio piquito porque me están ahogando y no dejan a mi agua seguir su curso.

Pero Mediopollito le contestó:

Voy al palacio a ver al rey;

no tengo tiempo que perder.

Y *tip tap, tip tap,* siguió muy de prisa su camino.

A poco andar, Mediopollito se encontró con un fuego que estaba a punto de apagarse.

–Mediopollito -le dijo el fuego-, ayúdame. Busca unas ramas secas con tu medio piquito y me las traes, para que no me muera.

Pero Mediopollito le contestó:

Voy al palacio a ver al rey;

no tengo tiempo que perder.

Y *tip tap, tip tap,* siguió muy de prisa su camino.

Más adelante, Mediopollito se encontró con el viento enredado en unas matas.

–Mediopollito -le dijo el viento-, ayúdame. Aparta estas matas con tu medio piquito para que yo pueda seguir soplando.

Pero Mediopollito le contestó:

Voy al palacio a ver al rey;

no tengo tiempo que perder.

Y *tip tap, tip tap,* siguió muy de prisa su camino.

Por fin, Mediopollito llegó al palacio.

–Ahora podré ver al rey -dijo muy contento.

Pero en ese mismo momento, el coci-

nero de palacio lo vio, lo cogió del pescuezo y se lo llevó a la cocina.

–Justo lo que necesitaba. Al rey le apetece consomé de pollo para la cena -dijo el cocinero y metió a Mediopollito en una cacerola de agua.

–¡Agua! ¡Agua! -chilló Mediopollito-. ¡Ayúdame que me estoy ahogando!

Pero el agua le contestó:

–Yo era el arroyo, las malezas me estaban ahogando y tú no quisiste ayudarme entonces. No te ayudaré yo ahora.

El cocinero encendió el fuego.

–¡Fuego! ¡Fuego! -chilló Mediopollito-.

¡Ayúdame que me estoy quemando!

Pero el fuego le contestó:

–Yo me estaba muriendo y tú no quisiste ayudarme entonces. Pues no te ayudaré yo ahora.

Mediopollito ya se estaba quemando, cuando pasó el viento. Se metió en la olla como un remolino, levantó en el aire a Mediopollito y lo sacó de la cocina.

–Gracias, viento -dijo Mediopollito-. Ya puedes dejarme en tierra.

Pero el viento le contestó:

–Yo estaba enredado en unas matas y tú no quisiste ayudarme. Entonces no te ayudaré yo ahora.

Y el viento sopló con mucha fuerza y elevó a Mediopollito hasta la punta del campanario. Allí lo dejó.

Y hasta el día de hoy ahí se le puede ver, en la veleta, con su única patica y su única alita, espiando con su único ojito a ver de qué lado viene el viento.

La Cucarachita Martínez

Un día, barriendo la acera enfrente de su casa, la Cucarachita Martínez se encontró una moneda. Se puso entonces muy contenta a pensar:

"¿Qué me compraré con esta moneda? ¿Qué me compraré? ¿Caramelos? ¿Dulce de leche? ¿Bombones? No, no, porque son golosinas. Mejor será que me compre un vestido de color guayaba".

Y así decidido, la Cucarachita Martínez se guardó la moneda en el bolsillo y siguió barriendo. Barre que te barre, se encontró otra moneda. ¡Qué sorpresa!

"¿Qué me compraré con esta moneda? ¿Qué me compraré? ¿Chocolates? ¿Jalea de piña? ¿Dulce de higos? No, no, porque son golosinas. Mejor será que me compre una cinta morada".

Y así decidido, la Cucarachita Martínez guardó la moneda y siguió barriendo la acera.

Barre que te barre, encontró otra moneda. ¡Qué maravilla!

"¿Qué me compraré con esta moneda? Ay, ¿qué me compraré? ¿Conservas de coco? ¿Jalea de mango? ¿Maní acaramelado? No, no, porque son golosinas. Mejor será que me compre una caja de polvo de olor".

Y así decidido, la Cucarachita Martínez se fue a la tienda a comprarse el vestido, la cinta y los polvos de olor. Regresó a su casa, se bañó, se empolvó, se puso el vestido nuevo y la cinta en el pelo. Luego, se sentó muy preciosa en la puerta de su casa.

Pasó por allí el toro y le dijo:

–Cucarachita Martínez, ¡qué linda estás!

–Si tú lo dices, así será -contestó la cucarachita con una dulce voz.

Y el toro, muy emocionado, le propuso:

–Cucarachita, ¿te quieres casar conmigo?

–¿Y cómo harás tú por la noche antes de dormirnos? -preguntó la cucarachita.

–*¡Muuuuu! ¡Muuuuu!* -bramó el toro con todas sus fuerzas.

–Ay, no, no, no, que me asustarás -contestó la cucarachita-. No, toro, no me casaré contigo.

Y el toro se fue, triste y descompuesto.

Luego, pasó por allí el perro y le dijo:

–Cucarachita Martínez, ¡qué linda estás!

–Si tú lo dices, así será -contestó la cucarachita con una dulce voz.

Y el perro, muy emocionado, le propuso:

–Cucarachita, ¿te quieres casar conmigo?

–¿Y cómo harás tú antes de dormirnos? -preguntó la cucarachita.

–*¡Guauuuu! ¡Guauuuu!* -ladró el perro con todas sus fuerzas.

–Ay, no, no, no, que me asustarás -contestó la cucarachita-. No, perro, no me casaré contigo.

Y el perro se fue, muy triste y con el rabo entre las piernas.

Pasó entonces por allí el gallo y le dijo:

–Cucarachita Martínez, ¡qué linda estás!

–Si tú lo dices, así será -contestó la cucarachita con una dulce voz.

Y el gallo, muy emocionado, le propuso:

–Cucarachita, ¿te quieres casar conmigo?

–¿Y cómo harás tú por la noche antes de dormirnos? -preguntó la cucarachita.

–*¡Kikirikiii! ¡Kikirikiii!* -cantó el gallo con todas sus fuerzas.

–Ay, no, no, no, que me asustarás -contestó la cucarachita-. No, gallo, no me casaré contigo.

Y el gallo se fue, muy triste y con la cresta ladeada.

Ya estaba oscureciendo, cuando pasó por allí el Ratón Pérez.

–Cucarachita Martínez, ¡qué bellísima estás!

–Si tú lo dices, así será -contestó la cucarachita con una dulce voz.

Y el Ratón Pérez, muy enamorado, le propuso:

–Cucarachita, ¿te quieres casar conmigo?

–¿Y cómo harás tú por la noche antes de dormirnos? -preguntó la cucarachita.

–*Chiii...chiii...chiii...* y quererte así -dijo muy bajito el Ratón Pérez y le dio un beso a la cucarachita.

Eso le gustó a la cucarachita y se casó con el Ratón Pérez.

Al día siguiente de la boda, la cucarachita fue al mercado y le encargó al Ratón Pérez que vigilara la olla que tenía en el fuego.

–Recuerda revolver la sopa de vez en

cuando, pero hazlo con el cucharón -le advirtió la cucarachita y se fue.

El ratón era muy goloso y quiso ver qué se estaba cocinando que olía tan sabroso. Olvidó lo que la cucarachita había recomendado y, en lugar del cucharón, tomó una cuchara pequeñita y se encaramó en la olla. ¡Era un hervido! Se veía delicioso y muy cerca flotaba una cebolla doradita.

Ratón Pérez trató de alcanzarla con la cucharita, pero estaba muy lejos. Se estiró, se estiró, se tambaleó, se tambaleó y *¡plun!* cayó dentro de la olla. ¡Pobre Ratón Pérez! Ahí mismo se ahogó.

Cuando la cucarachita regresó del mercado, buscó al Ratón Pérez por toda la casa. Buscó en la sala, buscó en el cuarto, buscó en el baño y no lo pudo encontrar. Finalmente, fue a la cocina y al revolver la olla, se dio cuenta de lo que había pasado.

Llorando, la cucarachita salió a la puerta de su casa y se puso a cantar:

El Ratón Pérez se cayó en la olla

por la golosina de la cebolla

y la cucarachita le canta y lo llora.

De cómo Ratón Pérez resucitó

La Cucaracha Martínez no podía consolarse de la muerte de Ratón Pérez y lloraba sentada en la puerta de su casa.

Pasó un pajarito y le preguntó:

-Cucarachita, ¿por qué lloras?

Y la cucarachita, muy triste, suspiró:

Porque Ratón Pérez
se cayó en la olla
por la golosina
de la cebolla.

Entonces el pajarito se cortó el piquito.

Volando, volando, el pajarito se encontró con una paloma que le preguntó:

–Pajarito, ¿por qué te cortaste el piquito?

Y el pajarito, muy triste, respondió:

Porque Ratón Pérez

se cayó en la olla

por la golosina

de la cebolla

y la cucarachita

suspira y llora.

Entonces la paloma se cortó la cola.

Fue la paloma a beber agua a la fuente y la fuente le preguntó:

–Paloma, ¿por qué te cortaste la cola?

Y la paloma, muy triste, respondió:

Porque el pajarito
se cortó el piquito
porque Ratón Pérez
se cayó en la olla
por la golosina
de la cebolla
y la cucarachita
suspira y llora.

Entonces la fuente secó su corriente.

Vino Ramón a buscar agua a la fuente y al verla seca, le preguntó:

–Fuente, ¿por qué secaste tu corriente?

Y la fuente, muy triste, respondió:

Porque la paloma

se cortó la cola

porque el pajarito

se cortó el piquito

porque Ratón Pérez

se cayó en la olla

por la golosina

de la cebolla

y la cucarachita

suspira y llora.

Entonces Ramón rompió su jarrón.

Cuando regresó a casa, la señora le preguntó:

-Ramón, ¿por qué rompiste tu jarrón?

Y Ramón, muy triste, respondió:

Porque la fuente

secó su corriente

porque la paloma

se cortó la cola

porque el pajarito

se cortó el piquito

porque Ratón Pérez

se cayó en la olla

por la golosina

de la cebolla

y la cucarachita

suspira y llora.

Entonces dijo la señora:

–Esto lo arreglamos ahora.

Y se fue corriendo con Ramón a buscar al doctor. La paloma y el pajarito iban volando atrás.

El doctor tomó su maletín y siguieron corriendo a casa de la cucarachita. Entre todos sacaron a Ratón Pérez de la olla, lo lavaron, lo acostaron y le dieron masajes con aceite de coco. El doctor le tomó el pulso y le puso unas gotas amargas en la boca. Entonces, Ratón Pérez estornudó y abrió los ojos.

En cuanto la cucarachita vio que Ratón Pérez se había salvado, fue a la cocina y preparó una olla de engrudo. Al pajarito, le pegó el piquito; a la paloma, le pegó la cola y a Ramón, le

arregló el jarrón.

¿Y el doctor? Recetó alcanfor.

¿Y la señora? Se compró una lora.

¿Y la fuente? Echó agua y cantó lo siguiente:

Este cuento se acabó;

entró por un callejón plateado

y salió por otro dorado.

Versos

La rata planchadora

Una rata vieja,
que era planchadora,
por planchar su falda
se quemó la cola.

Se puso pomada,
se amarró un pañito,
y en lugar de cola
le quedó un rabito.

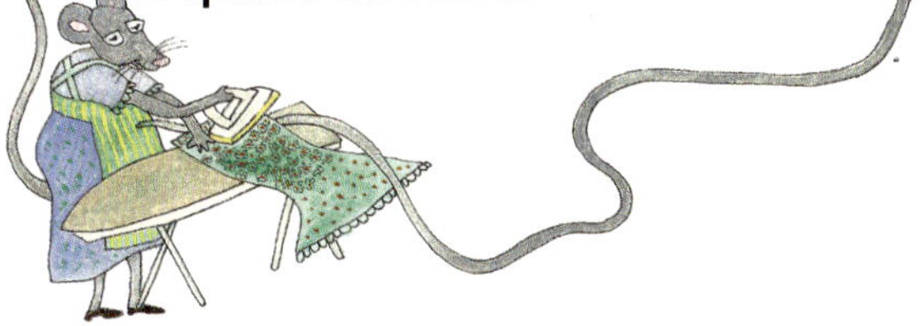

Los veinte ratones

Arriba y abajo
por los callejones,
pasa una ratita
con veinte ratones.

Unos sin colita
y otros muy colones;
unos sin orejas
y otros orejones.

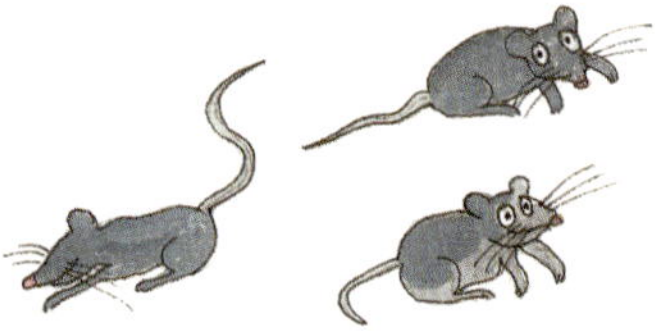

Unos sin paticas
y otros muy patones;
unos sin ojitos
y otros muy ojones.

Unos sin narices
y otros narizones;
unos sin dienticos
y otros muy dentones.

María Josefa

–María Josefa,
¡ven a barrer!
–No tengo manos,
no tengo pies.

–María Josefa,
¡ven a coser!
–No tengo manos,
no tengo pies.

–María Josefa,
¡ven a moler!
–No tengo manos,
no tengo pies.

–María Josefa,
¡ven a comer!
–Ya tengo manos,
ya tengo pies.

Pimpirigaña

Pimpirigaña
vino la araña
pidiendo un misal
para ir a rezar.

Pimpirigoma
llegó la paloma
pidiendo la sal
para cocinar.

Pimpiriguilla
vino la ardilla
pidiendo un lazo
de seda y raso.

Pimpirigallo
vino el caballo
pidiendo un real
para ir a comprar.

Pimpirigato
llegó el araguato
pidiendo limones,
bananas, melones.

AEIOU

Abeja
La abeja Alfonsina
anda sola y afligida:
–Busco un novio elegante,
sólo quiero al...

...Elefante
El elefante Juan José
suspirando toma el té:
–La abeja es una enana,
sólo quiero a la...

...Iguana

La iguana Isolina
mordisquea una semilla:
–El elefante es buenmozo pero
sólo quiero al...

...Oso

El oso Oscar la ha oído:
–Esa iguana, ¡qué fastidio!
cada vez está más flaca,
sólo quiero a la...

...Urraca

La urraca Ulderica
hace tortas y torticas
para Oscar y Alfonsina
Isolina y Juan José.

A E I O U
¿A cuál de ellos quieres tú?

Acerca de los cuentos

Hay historias que viajan por el mundo con gracia y ligereza; al correr de los años, se van incorporando a la tradición oral y escrita de los pueblos por donde pasan. Así ha sucedido con los breves cuentos de este libro venidos de Europa y avencindados en América. Están reunidos siete de los más populares que guardan la esencia de la tradición europea pero han asimilado el sabor criollo. La selección se realizó pensando en los niños pequeños para que los padres o abuelos se los lean, porque hay pocas cosas más deliciosas que escuchar un buen cuento leído con cariño.

A continuación, unas brevísimas notas acerca de cada una de las historias recogidas en este libro:

Ricitos de Oro tiene origen en un antiguo cuento escocés de una zorra que entra sin permiso a la casa de unos osos, come su comida, se sienta en sus sillas y duerme en sus camas. Con el tiempo, la zorra se transformó en una anciana y más tarde, en una niña que tenía un brillante cabello de plata; finalmente, en algunas versiones, la protagonista pasó a tener los rubios bucles con los que la conocemos hoy.

Los Siete Chivitos se encuentra en la recopilación de los hermanos Grimm con el nombre de *El lobo y los siete cabritillos.* La historia ha permanecido prácticamente igual, incluyendo el detalle de las patas enharinadas y el chivito pequeño que se esconde en la caja del reloj para salvarse del lobo.

Los Tres Cochinitos tiene su antecedente en una historia publicada en Inglaterra en 1813. En ella, el mayor de tres gansos engaña a la zorra que quiere comérselos construyendo una sólida casa de ladrillos. Hay también una antigua versión italiana en la que los protagonistas son tres ocas.

Mediopollito es un cuento español muy conocido en el País Vasco. En la versión original, Mediopollito encuentra una bolsa de dinero escarbando en el gallinero. El hijo del rey que pasaba por allí, se la pide prestada y nunca se la devuelve. La presente versión tiene un desarrollo diferente en muchos aspectos, pero es una de las más conocidas de América.

La Cucarachita Martínez es un cuento de origen andaluz. La protagonista es una hormiga coqueta que se enamora de un insecto llamado *ratompérez* en Andalucía. Con los años, el insecto pasó a ser el Ratón Pérez y en los países del Caribe, la hormiguita terminó siendo una cucarachita de apellido Martínez.

De cómo Ratón Pérez resucitó es una seguidilla del cuento anterior que suaviza el triste final. A veces, aparece como un epílogo de *La cucarachita Martínez.*

Desconocemos las fuentes de **La Gallinita Roja,** pero su estructura y la intención moralizante podrían indicar que tiene origen en una fábula.

V.U.

Verónica Uribe ha publicado numerosas adaptaciones de los cuentos y versos de la tradición oral, entre las cuales destaca *El libro de oro de los cuentos de hadas* y *El libro de oro de las fábulas.* Es autora de *Diego y los limones mágicos, Diego y el barco pirata, Diego y la gran cometa voladora* y de la novela juvenil *Tres buches de agua salada.*

Carmen Salvador es licenciada en arquitectura. Ha realizado estudios en la Escuela de Artes Visuales Cristóbal Rojas y en el Instituto de Arte Federico Brandt en Caracas. Sus libros para niños incluyen: *Estaba el señor Don Gato* y *El rey mocho.*

Bibliografía

Bettelheim, Bruno.
Psicoanálisis de los cuentos de hadas. Barcelona: Editorial Crítica, 1978.

Carpenter, Humphrey y Mary Pritchard.
The Oxford Companion to Children's Literature. Oxford: Oxford University Press, 1987.

Almodóvar, A.R.
Cuentos al amor de la lumbre. Madrid: Ediciones Generales Anaya, 1984.

Grimm, J. y W.
Cuentos de niños y del hogar. Madrid: Ediciones Generales Anaya, 1985.

Opie, Iona y Peter.
The Classic Fairy Tales. Nueva York: Oxford University Press, 1980.

EDICIONES
ekaré

Edición a cargo de Elena Iribarren
Dirección de Arte: Irene Savino

Tercera edición, 2005

Edif. Banco del Libro, Av. Luis Roche, Altamira Sur,
Caracas 1062, Venezuela · www.ekare.com

ISBN 980-257-133-4 · HECHO EL DEPÓSITO DE LEY
Depósito Legal lf1511998800787